The Education of Feeling and Emotion

Introductory Studies in Philosophy of Education
Series Editors: PHILIP SNELDERS and
COLIN WRINGE

Education and the Value of Knowledge by
M. A. B. Degenhardt
Can We Teach Children To Be Good? by Roger Straughan
Means and Ends in Education by Brenda Cohen
Mixed Ability Grouping: A Philosophical Perspective by
Charles Bailey and David Bridges

The Education of Feeling and Emotion

FRANCIS DUNLOP

London
GEORGE ALLEN & UNWIN
Boston   Sydney

George Allen & Unwin (Publishers) Ltd,
40 Museum Street, London WC1A 1LU, UK

George Allen & Unwin (Publishers) Ltd,
Park Lane, Hemel Hempstead, Herts HP2 4TE, UK

Allen & Unwin, Inc.,
9 Winchester Terrace, Winchester, Mass. 01890, USA

George Allen & Unwin Australia Pty Ltd,
8 Napier Street, North Sydney, NSW 2060, Australia

First published in 1984

British Library Cataloguing in Publication Data

Dunlop, F.
    The education of feeling and emotion. —
(Introductory studies in philosophy of education)
1. Emotions
I. Title   II. Series
152.4   BF531
ISBN 0-04-370132-9
ISBN 0-04-370133-7 Pbk

Library of Congress Cataloging in Publication Data applied for

Set in 10 on 11 point Plantin by Grove Graphics, Tring, Hertfordshire
and printed in Great Britain
by Biddles Ltd, Guildford, Surrey

Contents

Editors' Foreword

Books that are available to students of philosophy of education may, in general, be divided into two types. There are collections of essays and articles making up a more or less random selection; and there are books which explore a single theme or argument in depth but, having been written to break new ground, are often unsuitable for general readers or those near the beginning of their course. The Introductory Studies in Philosophy of Education are intended to fill what is widely regarded as an important gap in this range.

The series aims to provide a collection of short, readable works which, besides being philosophically sound, will seem relevant and accessible to future and existing teachers without a previous knowledge of philosophy or of philosophy of education. In the planning of the series account has necessarily been taken of the tendency of present-day courses of teacher education to follow a more integrated and less discipline-based pattern than formerly. Account has also been taken of the fact that students on three- and four-year courses, as well as those on shorter postgraduate and in-service courses, quite understandably expect their theoretical studies to have a clear bearing on their practical concerns, and on their dealings with children. Each book, therefore, starts from a real and widely recognised problem in the educational field, and explores the main philosophical approaches which illuminate and clarify it, or suggests a coherent standpoint even when it does not claim to provide a solution. Attention is paid to the work of both mainstream philosophers and philosophers of education. For students who wish to pursue particular questions in depth, each book contains a bibliographical essay or a substantial list of suggestions for further reading. It is intended that a full range of the main topics recently discussed by philosophers of education should eventually be covered by the series.

Besides having considerable experience in the teaching of philosophy of education, the majority of authors writing in the series have already received some recognition in their particular fields. In addition, therefore, to reviewing and criticising existing work, each author has his or her own positive contribution to make to further discussion.

PHILIP SNELDERS
COLIN WRINGE

1

Introductory

If we were asked to describe the sort of person we would be most frightened of, we might well think of a man whose intellectual powers were outstanding and properly trained but who had no 'heart' and no feelings. Such a person, we might think, would be capable of any enormity. Indeed, we might well be tempted to say that he was not a person at all but a non-human monster in human form. Science fiction writers and horror film makers have long known how to exploit such facts. They testify to the absolutely central importance of emotion and feeling in human life.

We may also recall occasions when we have heard people say about their children's education: 'I don't care how clever he is, or how many qualifications he gets out of school. As long as his heart's in the right place he won't go far wrong.' It is also a fact that parents and educational writers have constantly criticised schools for failing to put the 'hearts' of their pupils 'in the right place', or – in modern terms – for failing to educate their emotions. There can be no doubt of the very great importance of affective education.

It is a striking fact that, whereas the cognitive or intellectual components of education are usually first thought of in terms of achievements, the emotional or affective components are normally thought of first in terms of deficiencies. Whether this is an accident of our own civilisation, or whether there is something in the very nature of human life and experience that encourages this, may or may not emerge later, but here we simply recall the familiar facts. The acquisition of knowledge, of ways of looking at things, of theoretical procedures and methods, of concepts, languages and forms of discourse – all these achievements are common currency among teachers, and frequently discussed in philosophical and other writings on education. But when we come to the 'heart', to emotions and feelings, to the 'affective' sphere in general, what we normally hear about and talk of are the symptoms

1

of lack of achievement, or of possible failure on somebody's part – of apathy, self-centredness, emotional volatility and over-excitability, sentimentality, inauthenticity, emotional disorder and 'crudity', of coldness, repression, lack of self-control and self-knowledge. There is far less mention of affective *achievements*, and very little discussion of the field in comparison with other aspects of education.

This is partly because of the inherent difficulties of the task. Emotion and feeling are extremely hard to talk about systematically. There is great imprecision and looseness in the ordinary language used to refer to them, and the approaches of those few writers who have tried to discuss them at some length vary to a surprising extent. One constantly finds oneself wondering whether they are even talking about the same thing at all. It is also because the phenomena are highly obscure and elusive 'in themselves', as will become apparent below. It is thus not surprising that the *education* of feeling and emotion should be a rather neglected topic.

The main task of this book, then, will be to try and bring about an understanding of what this might involve, and of why it is so important. This will entail analysing not the *language* (or *concepts*) of emotion – for this, as I have said, is in considerable disarray, and the method of conceptual analysis is thus hard to employ very fruitfully – but emotional and affective experience itself. The analysis, in other words, will be more 'phenomenological' than 'conceptual'. It will also lead inevitably to a consideration of human nature in general, and to an examination of the place of the feelings and emotions in the 'human economy'.

But in this introductory chapter I should perhaps say something about the concept of education. It seems clear enough to me that the word 'education' is one whose meaning changes with the context and with the purposes of the user. This is because when the word is used to refer to the educative *activities* or *policies* of parents and teachers, their inevitably differing conceptions of the task of preparing children for adult life impart different connotations to the word itself. There is little point in trying to tie it firmly down to one clearly defined meaning, or even in trying to argue that one's own use should become the standard use. But a philosophical examination of feeling and emotion makes it very clear to my mind that 'affective' education, at least, will have to be understood largely in terms of development. As I shall point out later there certainly *are* non-developmental issues that arise in the field. There is, for instance, the general question of what teachers can legitimately do about (or ought to do about) their pupils' eventual *policy* with regard to feeling in their lives. 'Life-styles', in other words, can be partly characterised in terms of the place they offer to feeling and emotion. But the basic educational task must be seen in developmental terms, and this is how I shall normally be understanding it.

The teacher's task can normally be taken to cover at least three sorts of things:

(1) what he directly tells or teaches children, or deliberately tells them to learn;
(2) what he hopes to bring about indirectly in his pupils by the deliberate or planned provision of a particular sort of physical environment, psychological atmosphere, classroom organisation, and so on;
(3) what he hopes will 'rub off' on pupils as a result of his being the person he is. What I have in mind here are the sorts of things that are said to be 'caught', not 'taught', and over which the teacher has little, if any, direct control (at least in the short term).

It will become apparent that a great deal of what comes under the heading of affective education is transmitted, encouraged, or sparked off in the last two sorts of way. It might thus be said that the 'curriculum' of emotional education is largely – and has largely to remain – a 'hidden' one.

Since there will not be much about 'justification' in this book, I had better make a few brief remarks about it here. It seems to me that if one can show that affective education is largely a matter of development as a human being, or as a person, and that this process cannot take place automatically but requires the help and guidance of others, then one has provided all the 'justification' for affective education that one need provide. For who could doubt that, other things being equal, it is better to be a developed person than an undeveloped one? It is arguable that it is, in any case, the philosopher's job to illuminate and clarify, rather than to justify. This can be left to moralists and advocates.

But it might perhaps be objected that largely 'hidden' curricula were always suspect, and that it was *this* aspect of what I call affective education that needed justifying. But the 'hiddenness' of curricula is inevitable. For example, we would all agree that children should be taught their native language. But children can have no conception that in learning to speak they are learning to see the world and to evaluate it in ways they have not dreamt of, and which would have been different had they been brought up in a different culture (see below, Chapter 5). There is thus something essentially arbitrary and 'hidden' about learning one's native tongue. But if children are not taught *any* language for fear of indoctrination they will hardly become human at all in any but the most rudimentary respects. All human being, from the moment of conception, is riddled with arbitrariness and contingency. Had we not been born (I speak to readers in the United Kingdom) in this country, in this century, our chances of being educated *at all* beyond a very elementary level would have been small. The 'hiddenness' of curricula is an essential component of the arbitrary 'conditions' that make persons what they are.

One last point must be briefly discussed here. I do not in the least wish to imply that I think teachers or schools can fully achieve the affective education of their pupils. Common sense and traditional wisdom suggest that some aspects of it at least are within their range. But various factors may clearly also prevent the attainment of others, among them the following:

(1) Innate limitations of pupils. For example, it is normally taken for granted that pupils vary in sensitivity. It seems extremely likely that some of this variation – the same goes for other relevant capacities – is due to hereditary factors.

(2) The extreme importance of the pre-school years and, in particular, the relationship with the mother. It may be that where the young child has never received much love and affection before he comes to school, his chances of attaining affective maturity through formal education are very small.

(3) Anti-educational factors in the child's social environment. These may, for example, lead to his rejection of 'school' and of all that it stands for, and to a neutralising of the teacher's own unplanned and possible unconscious influence.

(4) 'Maturational' factors. It may be that some aspects of affective education will be achieved in a given child whatever teachers do or refrain from doing (at any rate, within the limits of what we would normally expect from a teacher).

In other words, some of our aims in affective education may be unrealistic or pointless in regard to some children, and others may be so in regard to all. The fact is that we simply do not know the extent to which the school is capable of bringing about education of the emotions. But then *all* education is a chancy business, still largely – despite vast sums spent on research – a hit-or-miss undertaking. This should really not surprise us, given the nature of human beings and above all the presence in them of free will and essentially limited vision. Indeed, we should, in my view, be far more worried if education was *not* a chancy business, since this would suggest that children really had been reduced to so much 'raw material'.

However, although I shall be addressing myself to practical questions in the last part of this book, I want to make it clear that its prime purpose is to help people understand what emotions and feelings are, and what part they play in the 'economy' of human life. Given this understanding, a person may begin to get an idea of what education of the emotions might be, and thus approach the practical questions in an objective and realistic frame of mind. Even if many of them may still seem uncertain of solution one will, thus fortified, have advanced several steps towards it.

2

Two Preliminary Accounts: R. S. Peters and John MacMurray

I turn now to discuss the work on emotion and emotional education of R. S. Peters and John MacMurray. Their contributions are not only important in themselves, but also serve to open up the subject for us. Having looked in detail at these two philosophers' work I shall go on to address the theme of this book, topic by topic, in a more general way.

Although Peters and MacMurray have something in common, their main conclusions are very different. Peters's work, both as philosophical psychologist and as promoter of the philosophical study of education as a distinct discipline at all levels of educational study, has been enormously influential in this country, the Antipodes and now increasingly in North America. His work in various branches of philosophy of education still forms an almost indispensable starting-point for serious discussion. This is certainly true of our own topic. By contrast John MacMurray (b. 1891, d. 1976) is little studied in either mainstream philosophical or philosophy of education circles today, though his books of broadcast talks had large sales outside the universities before the Second World War. Perhaps this very fact helps to explain the lack of interest taken in him today in academic circles. Yet his *Reason and Emotion,* which contains a section on the education of the emotions, is important to our theme, and provides an extremely instructive contrast to the contribution of Richard Peters.

It may be helpful to give first a very brief sketch of the 'accepted view' on emotion in mainstream philosophy before Peters intervened. The 'traditional view' had accepted that emotions were a particular kind of experience. It was also generally agreed that these experiences, some kind of feelings, were connected to 'cognitions', to seeing things in certain

6

lights, as dangerous, threatening, and so on, and were typically connected to internal physiological changes and publicly observable expressive behaviour, but few, if any, doubted that emotion words (anger, fear, and so on) were the names of particular kinds of experience involving feeling. The 'revolution in philosophy' associated with Ryle, Wittgenstein and Austin changed all this. A key point was the challenging of the view that general words (ordinary nouns, adjectives, and so on) named types of 'object' (material, personal, or mental) or their qualities. In many quarters it became an article of faith that they never do. An aspect of this change was an interest in the process by which the meanings of words could be learnt, and the attempt to make all this luminously clear.

Errol Bedford was among the first to apply this new set of concerns to emotion. He argued, in a well-known paper (Bedford, 1956–7), that 'an emotion is not any sort of experience or process'. He did not deny that angry or irritated men experienced some sort of feeling, but made it clear that this fact was of no importance or significance, since, he claimed, it was not part of the job of emotion words to refer to feelings at all. Rather, they formed 'part of the vocabulary of appraisal and criticism', including moral criticism (p. 89). The crucial point in all this concerns feelings, and the question of whether we can introspectively make out a difference in quality between, say, indignation and annoyance (Bedford's example), or between anger and disgust (a better example), at least partly because these things feel different. Bedford not only denied this on the basis of self-examination but also argued that it *could* not be true, since, if it were, emotion words could not be learnt. If I set out to teach a child the meaning of 'anger', and 'anger' is primarily the name of a kind of subjective experience, then I shall never be able to do this, since I cannot be sure what kind of subjective experience the child is having at any particular moment. We shall return to this issue later.

The Views of R. S. Peters

Peters largely agrees with Bedford's insistence on the unimportance and independent unidentifiability of the feelings underlying emotions, and also with his stress on appraisals, but argues that he has ignored the common-sense association of emotion with 'passivity'. He also insists that emotions are 'states of mind'. His position thus represents a step back in the direction of the more traditional view. A good starting-point for an exposition of Peters's ideas is provided by his brief account in *The Logic of Education* (Hirst and Peters, 1970, pp. 49f.).

The central feature of states of mind which we call 'emotions', such as fear, jealousy, remorse, etc., is a type of cognition that can be called an appraisal. A situation is seen under an aspect which is pleasing or displeasing, beneficial or harmful. To feel fear, for instance, is to see a situation as dangerous; to feel pride is to see with pleasure something as ours or as something that we have had a hand in bringing about . . . The appraisal in each case has a feeling side to it. If fear is felt, seeing something as dangerous is different from seeing it as three feet high or as green, in that it is non-neutral. Green or something's height may, of course, in certain contexts contingently affect us powerfully; but it is not part of our understanding of these features of the environment that they should matter to us in this way. With features picked out by states of mind which we call emotions, on the other hand, the connection with feeling is a conceptual one. That is why the cognitive core of the emotion is referred to as an appraisal and not just as a judgment. But the feeling is inseparable from the cognition; we could not identify such feelings without reference to the understanding of the situations which evokes them.

Note here particularly the stress on cognition (it is 'the central feature' of emotions; they have a 'cognitive core') and the secondary and, presumably, more peripheral place of feeling, which is interpreted in terms of objects 'affecting' us or 'mattering' to us and, again, as having no qualities of its own (as, for example, colour does) which might enable us to identify what sort of feeling we are experiencing 'without reference to the understanding of the situations which evokes them'.

This fairly straightforward account gives way to a rather more complicated one when we turn to Peters's paper 'The education of the emotions' (1970). Part of this is a discussion of the common assumption that there is 'an intimate connection between emotion and "motivated behaviour" '. He is including here such views as that of Magda Arnold who defines emotion as 'a felt tendency towards or away from an object' preceded by an appraisal. Peters's reason for denying this 'conceptual connection' is that some emotions do not issue in any tendency to action. I shall discuss this argument below (pp. 13f).

But he also argues here (as he does in Peters, 1961–2) that another element besides an appraisal must be present before we are really entitled to talk of emotion. For words like 'envy' or 'jealousy' may simply indicate a person's *motive* in performing the particular action he did perform (for example, 'making damaging remarks about a colleague'). However (1970, p. 178):

We talk about jealousy as an *emotion* [my italics] . . . when a person is subject to unpleasant feelings that come over him when he views his colleague's behaviour in a certain light . . . The term 'emotion', in other words, is typically used in ordinary language to pick out our passivity. We speak of judgements being disturbed, warped, heightened, sharpened and clouded by emotion, of people being in command or not being properly in control of their emotions, being emotionally perturbed, upset, involved, excited and exhausted. In a similar vein, we speak of emotional states, upheavals, outbursts and reactions. The suggestion in such cases is that something comes over people or happens to them.

In fact, he goes on, neither 'motive' nor 'emotion'

pick[s] out, as it were, distinctive items in the furniture of the mind. I am claiming, on the contrary, that they are terms we employ when we wish to link the *same* mental acts of appraisal with *different* forms of behaviour – with actions on the one hand and with a variety of passive phenomena on the other. The appraisals involved, however, need not issue in either motives or emotions. We can say, 'I envy him his equanimity' or 'I am sorry that you can't come to stay', without acting in the light of the relevant appraisal and without being emotionally affected in any way.

Appraisals, then, are central to any account of emotion. But we can either 'connect these appraisals with things we *do*', in which case they 'function' as motives, or with 'things that *come over us*', in which case we talk of emotions. In 'strong cases of emotion' our passivity also takes a noticeably physical form (trembling, sweating, blushing, and so on). But (p. 179):

There is, too, the intermediary class of some reactions, which are typically of an unco-ordinated protopathic type, that spring from an intuitive, sometimes subliminal type of appraisal of a situation. An example would be when a person lashes out in anger or starts with fear. These are not reactions to stimuli, like jumping when one receives an electric shock, because of their cognitive core. Neither are they actions in a full-blown sense; for there is no grasp of means to ends, no consideration of possible ends of action. They are what we call 'emotional reactions'.

Later in the same paper Peters suggests that all emotional appraisals are like this (p. 182):

The more we think of . . . appraisals as *emotions* and hence stress our passivity with regard to them, the more we tend to think of the appraisals as immediate and 'intuitive', and of our reactions as veering towards the involuntary. 'Emotional reactions' illustrate both these features.

Peters divides the educational task into two parts: 'the development of appropriate appraisals' and 'the control and canalisation of passivity'. The first is primarily 'a moral matter', and consists largely in teaching children to make their appraisals more rational by teaching them the nature and use of appropriate 'moral and aesthetic criteria'. Teachers, however, would be wise to listen to psychologists as well as moralists and moral philosophers, since the former can perhaps produce evidence about what is possible in the way of refining emotions, or show the pervasive foundational importance of certain emotions in human life. But in general there is stress on the importance of linguistic and conceptual development, of fostering objectivity, insight, truthfulness and the ability to recognise emotion in oneself and others.

The section on the control and canalisation of passivity has three subsections. The first concerns the development of self-transcending emotions and their 'stabilisation' in 'sentiments' or 'settled disposition[s] to make appraisals of a certain sort'. As this is the most important way of preventing people from relating to the world in the childish, self-referential way characteristic of 'emotional reactions', it is, in effect, another way in which our lives can be made more rational. The second subsection is concerned with the development of 'appropriate action patterns'. In this way appraisals that before merely gave rise to symptoms of passivity become motives for appropriate action and thereby, presumably, bring more rational and less primitive cognitive activity in their train. The last part is concerned with 'the discharge of passivity through the expression of the emotions'. The presupposition here is that emotion must find some sort of outlet, so, in the case for example, of 'hate, fear and lust', it is important that individuals learn appropriate ways of expressing them in, for example, 'speech and symbolic gesture' to avoid the extremes of 'quivering in the passive state specific to the appraisals in question' and 'launching into the relevant actions of murder, flight and rape'. Expressive forms are thus 'intermediary' forms, lying halfway between passivity and action (p. 190). It is worth adding that Peters nowhere comments on the extreme oddness of this need to 'canalise' 'passivity'. It remains an unintelligible skeleton in the cupboard of his 'rational man'. But we shall meet his practical suggestions again in Chapter 5 below.

To complete our survey of Peters's account of emotion we must turn to his paper 'Reason and passion' he seems to regard 'passion' as a straightforward alternative to 'emotion' (Peters, 1971). He here rejects Hume's idea that 'reason is merely the ability to make inductive and deductive inferences whose basis is a "wonderful and unintelligible instinct" in the soul of the individual' (p. 156). On the contrary, he claims, it is 'essentially public', since it is 'an internalisation of public procedures' (p. 154).

How, then, is passion related to reason? He argues against the idea that reason goes with calm passions, but is incompatible with turbulent ones. Bertrand Russell's passion for truth 'was anything but calm'. He also discounts the idea that reason and passion are irreconcilable in any form, arguing that emotions or passions can be reasonable or rational (when based on rational appraisals), and that being unreasonable or even irrational does not necessarily imply passivity. Nevertheless he accepts – as we saw above – that emotion does *tend* to be irrational or unreasonable, though it need not be.

The main part of the paper is given up to a description of 'levels of life', which provide what Peters presents as a more satisfactory way of understanding the relation between reason and passion.

The lowest level of (human) life is that of 'irrationality', which is characteristic of infants and of aspects of the life of members of primitive societies. Here experience is not 'structured by categories of thought associated with reason' (p. 162). Life is dominated by non-rational wishes and aversions. Things are classified on the basis of subjectively felt similarities. Thinking thus 'manifests the combination of wish or aversion together with a low-grade form of classification and inference' (p. 163). 'Emotional reactions' are typical of this level of life and experience. The important point about all this is not that passion prevents reason from showing itself. Rather (p. 165):

> It is a case of a lapse from one level of conduct at which the perception of the situation is structured in terms of one group of passions being replaced by another level of reaction which also has its own cognitive and affective components.

What is lacking is not only objectivity and rational rule-following, but also those passions 'connected with the point of the activity in which the individual is engaged' and also 'the rational passions', such as concern for truth, relevance, procedural rules, etc. (p. 166).

The next level is that of 'unreasonableness', which 'is connected with a level of life where there are reasons, but the reasons are of a pretty low-grade sort'. It is associated with faulty socialisation, tending to be ' "sense-bound", to be swayed by pleasures and pains of the moment. Emotions, usually of a gusty sort, are aroused only by particular people and situations' (pp. 168f.).

The final level is that of 'the rational passions'. Here the abilities 'to infer, demonstrate, etc.' are fully supported by 'the concern for truth', which involves concern about correctness, consistency, clarity and sincerity, and an abhorrence of irrelevance 'and other forms of arbitrariness' (pp. 169f.). Although these passions obviously fit theoretical inquiries well, 'they are also involved in practical activities and judgements in so far as these are conducted in a rational manner', including those involved in 'the interpersonal and moral spheres' (pp. 170f.). The life of the rational man could thus be as passionate as the lives of the infant or primitive, and that of the 'unreasonable man'. The three types differ in the nature of their cognitive endeavours (only the first is properly rational) and in the nature of the emotions or passions to which they are typically subject.

Critique of R. S. Peters's Views

This picture is not as clear as one might wish. Anyone attempting to assess it is bound, I think, to involve himself in interpretation that is partly conjectural. Despite Peters's insistence that the rational man needs the rational passions, the general impression conveyed by the account is that emotion is by and large an untrustworthy thing that we would really be much better without. This theme is clearly expressed in the idea that the appraisals underlying emotion tend to be hasty, 'low-grade' and intuitive; the idea of passivity is predominantly associated – despite passages to the contrary – with disturbance and interference at the rational level. But, as I say, this is to talk of a 'general impression'.

What, then, of more detailed criticism? One problem concerns the role of feeling and its relation to passivity, both in motivated action and in emotion. Emotions are characterised as 'appraisals with a feeling side to them'. This is interpreted in these terms: certain things 'affect' us, 'matter' to us. Their cognition is thus not the same as that of indifferent states of affairs, giving rise to appraisals instead of judgements. But appraisals do not necessarily involve passivity, which would make them emotional. They can simply provide us with reasons for action and, under these circumstances, there is no passivity in the case. Indeed, they need not motivate either; we may merely appraise a situation . . . and leave it at that.

Do these non-emotional appraisals still have 'a feeling side'? Presumably they do or they would not be called appraisals. If so, we are still 'affected' by something. But is this not a form of passivity? Suppose I am present at an act of injustice. I turn aside and hasten away, intent on my business. I will not allow the unjust act to impinge on me, since, if I did, I might have to do something about it. True, I have somehow 'glimpsed' it. But I have not let it come home to me, have not let it affect me. Again, a man is in love with a girl, and hears that she has started seeing a lot of a colleague. He feels jealous and, as a result, starts to encourage others to retail slanderous gossip about him. But, in order for his perception of the situation to 'move' him, or 'provide him with a reason for action', he has to let it work on him. He could simply take no notice, or refuse to believe the evidence before him. Peters is right to say that appraisals involve being affected. But he surely ought to add that being affected is itself a form of passivity, even though it is preceded by a kind of consent.

Consider now his account of the rational passions. These really are supposed to be passions. In Russell's case, his passion for truth is said to have been 'turbulent'. But all passion, or emotion, involves passivity. And yet passivity in general is supposed to make it more likely that our appraisals will be hasty, or intuitive, not properly and rationally considered. 'Passivity' is the name for phenomena that 'come over us', that 'overwhelm' us, that we cannot, or can only with difficulty, control. Is this really the case with a concern for correctness, or accuracy, or an abhorrence of irrelevance? Is a man with a concern for truth actually less likely to attain it than one without it? How is this paradox to be solved?

It seems to me that letting things impinge on one, or being affected by things, is a different phenomenon from being overwhelmed, or losing control. The latter is not common among rational people – yet the former is extremely common. It is certainly true that a person who is swept away by rage or exasperation, and bursts out in an 'ungovernable' passion, has in some sense 'consented' to this. We have to 'let go', to abdicate our responsibility for ourselves, to reach this state. Human experience is the experience of free will. We *can* 'let ourselves go', but this is to some extent a free act. Thus both forms of passivity involve consent. But there is an important difference between letting oneself be swept away, and letting oneself be affected and 'motivated'. We do not really continue to *act* in the first sort of case at all, since it is precisely our agency that we have surrendered. But though there is certainly passivity in acting out of jealousy, or love, and so on, we are still indubitably agents.

The effect of these considerations is to break down Peters's distinction between appraisals that motivate and appraisals accompanied by passivity, and to reinstate the very widely held view that emotion and action (or motive to action) are essentially connected. Peters argues that this is based on a confusion, and appeals to the following considerations designed to refute the claim: 'One cannot act in an appropriate way out of wonder or grief; one is overwhelmed by them' (1970, p. 179). This seems to me to be simply false. For example: I step out of my country cottage at night and look up at the clear starry sky. Deeply stirred by the wonder of it all, I am moved to utter a prayer of thanks to God for the glories of creation. Or again, I hear the news that a very dear friend has died. Full of grief, I decide to cancel my evening engagement. These seem to me to be completely appropriate actions that one may perform out of wonder and grief respectively. It may be as well here to comment on Peters's discounting of mourning rituals as coming within the category of 'appropriate action'. Peters rejects this because ritual is expressive; to count as action proper, and hence to be the sort of thing one could have a 'motive' to perform, action must involve taking means to an end. This seems highly stipulative. But in any case the point of insisting on the necessary link between emotion and motive (or action) may not be to establish a link between emotion and taking practical means to an end – they are supposed, says Peters, to 'remedy or retain what is unpleasant or pleasant about the situation which is appraised' (1970, p. 179) – but between emotion as an experience and some kind of behavioural response. Apart from this, what we call expressive action (mourning rituals and so on) certainly does have a practical function in the 'emotional economy' of the person's life, and serves various ends that the actor may dimly sense.

A much more controversial question about Peters's theory concerns his account of the relation between reason and passion and, in particular, his account of the nature of reason. Reason is said to be 'an internalisation of public procedures – those of criticism, the production of counter-examples, and the suggestion of different points of view' (1971, p. 154). This is a vital question because, although Peters accepts that reason needs passion, his account of appraisals and their development makes it clear that reason would really prefer to get by with as little passion as possible, since passion and even the 'rational passions' – at any rate, we are given no reason to believe the contrary – affect appraisals, making them precisely less rational. So it becomes important to inquire where reason comes from. What, in other words, is the ultimate origin of these 'public procedures' that the individual has primarily to conform to?

Peters admits (loc. cit.) that reason

has its origin in the primitive tendency manifest in intelligence to 'accommodate' or to change assumptions because the differences encountered in a novel situation do not permit assimilation, or the fitting of it within existing assumptions. But in reasoning proper, this caution born of the frequent experience of being in error because of the differences between situations, becomes the principle enunciated by Francis Bacon that a search must always be made for the negative instance . . . There must also be some form of public test to decide between competing assumptions.

14

The paragraph ends with a short eulogy of science as 'the supreme example of reason in action'.

The admission that reason originates in 'a primitive tendency' is important. Such tendencies are feelings that we all experience every day. We step outside the house one morning, unlock the garage, start backing the car out, but feel that something is wrong. We stop, and allow the thought to surface and impinge on us that our brief-case is not in its usual place on the seat beside us. Reading quickly through a pupil's essay we feel uneasy. Something is not quite as it should be. We carefully read the passage again and detect a logical howler. We have been used to the assumption that a certain middle-aged lady of our acquaintance is unmarried. In conversation with her one day we suddenly feel, on the basis of something 'she must have said', that our assumption was mistaken, and we start consciously looking for signs that she is widowed or divorced. These 'primitive tendencies' underlying reason manifest themselves in consciousness as feelings – feelings of unease when we cannot assimilate and of pressure to 'look again', of relief or of satisfaction when we succeed in accommodating.

If this is so then the 'caution' Peters talks about can only become 'the principle enunciated by Francis Bacon' in a provisional or 'rule of thumb' sense. It is possible to argue that the 'search for the negative instance' is not always a particularly helpful principle in science – certainly not one that should be exalted over other principles. Michael Polanyi instances many cases where, had that principle been regarded as completely authoritative, the progress of science would have been gravely impeded (e.g. 1973, p. 20). The fact is that it is extremely difficult to translate the feelings, hunches and intuitions scientists actually rely on, and upon which 'scientific reason' is based, into *any* really helpful set of principles that an individual could be explicitly taught. Scientists and philosophers disagree considerably about the 'public procedures' of 'scientific reason'; the activity of scientific discovery meanwhile proceeds serenely on its way. Scientists, in Polanyi's terms, know 'more than they can say'. Their knowledge is 'tacit', largely a matter of feeling their way (1973, *passim*).

There is thus *no* need for there to be 'some form of public test to decide between competing assumptions', if by that is meant some 'objective' and 'impersonal' court of appeal or set of procedures that simply have to be 'followed' to get the answer. 'Public tests', in so far as they do exist, are suggestions, hints, rough indications, with limited and provisional validity, that may be found useful in one case but not in another. If this is true of science, as Polanyi and others have cogently argued, how much more is it likely to be the case in the moral, interpersonal, or religious spheres? The search for 'testing procedures [that] . . . guarantee objectivity' is a chimerical one.

15

The origin of 'principles of reason' in feeling is given eloquent defence in the language that naturally occurs to us in talking about them. Peters himself writes of 'some assessment of the comparative *strength* of considerations', of reasons being '*very weak*', of a man having 'a very limited view of what considerations are *of most weight*', of an individual's ends being '*more important*', of certain ends of human action being '(in)*conceivable*', and so on (my italics in every case). None of this is explained. The first three characterisations, with their physical metaphors, are most naturally and easily explained in terms of the 'strength' of feeling, the 'feeling side' which is an inextricable part of appraisals. From 'importance' to 'weightiness' it is but a small step, and once more we are back with the strength of feeling. The conceivability of ends might be thought to be a different matter, involving a totally different psychic faculty. But there are close connections between imagination and feeling (see below, p. 68), and we will not go far wrong in assuming that human ends are 'conceivable' not when, as some philosophers claim, they do not involve any 'logical' inconsistency, but when we can 'feel' them as 'possible' ends for ourselves.

We may note too − the matter will be discussed more fully below − that Peters gives no hint as to how the 'appropriateness' of feelings in general is to be interpreted. Certainly there are logical points connected with the meanings of emotion words. You cannot, logically, say you are 'proud' of something unconnected with yourself, or irritated with someone unless he has thwarted or displeased you, and so on. But what does make the 'feeling side' of indignation rational when my friend has deceived me? (1971, p. 160). Peters does not say. But clearly we *could* try to train or condition people not to have such feelings. I suggest that we have to accept both that such feelings *are* appropriate − this is the lesson of ordinary interpersonal life − and that the 'justification' has something to do with the 'structure of feeling' itself (see below).

But, to return directly to the question of the origin of 'reason' within the person, Peters is certainly right to go on to say that 'it is most implausible to suggest that these critical procedures develop naturally in children's minds as they grow up' (understanding these procedures as rough rules of thumb − imperfect and often conflicting 'rationalisations' of countless acts of 'feeling one's way'). Children (at least when they are not geniuses) normally need to be taught. But that does not mean that they need to be given something wholly new to them, something that is not 'already there' in embryo. If rough procedural rules of thumb have their origin in primitive tendencies we should rather understand teaching as the development of something that is there 'in germ', the giving of *socially elaborated form* to dynamic questings and probings that are part of human nature. There is a vast social deposit of 'felt' ways of proceeding that can be handed on by example and personal contact. But this 'social deposit' is nothing without, and develops from, the tacit explorations of individuals. It is, in other words, feeling that has the logical priority. The assimilation of 'public rational procedures' is thus empty or merely 'scholastic' unless this assimilation is also a development of the basic repertoire of natural human feeling.

When Peters talks of appraisals as having 'a feeling side' to them, and goes on to say that these appraisals are judged for their 'appropriateness' in the light of 'moral and aesthetic criteria', we are being invited, I think, to adopt what Mary Midgley calls the 'colonial governor' model of reason (1978, p. 260); according to this, reason is the boss — it is its vocation to impose order on an unruly crowd of passions or feelings. We are now in a position to see that these 'criteria' may be themselves derived from feeling. This is a matter which we shall soon have to take up again.

Two other points must be briefly looked at here. We have seen that Peters accepts the view that the 'feeling side' of emotion is inseparable from the 'cognitive core', and that anger and disgust, say, could not be differentiated simply *as* feelings, or feeling-qualities, since otherwise emotion words could not be learnt. This argument is based on scepticism, and will be criticised properly below (pp. 51–2). But it is worth noting that Peters, in his account of emotion as passivity, talks of people 'being emotionally perturbed, upset, involved, excited and exhausted. In a similar vein', he continues, 'we speak of emotional states, upheavals, outbursts and reactions' (1970, p. 178). But what is the point of all these different terms unless at least some of them differentiate *qualities* of experience? For it is true that being emotionally perturbed feels different from being emotionally involved and again from being emotionally exhausted.

The other point concerns 'levels of life'. This is of enormous importance. Peters's description of the level of 'irrationality' has many excellent touches, but the phenomenon is an essential aspect of human being. Where he goes wrong is in his assumption that it is the task of the rational man to leave this level behind altogether. A much more adequate picture of levels and their relationship is described by Strasser and Lersch, whom we shall encounter below. Let me simply claim for the time being that a fully human life must at all times involve *all* or rather *both* layers (for Peters's level of 'unreasonableness' is merely a defective form of the life of the 'rational passions'). Human beings cannot remain human if they leave a great part of themselves behind.

The Views of John MacMurray

I turn now to consider MacMurray's views, which I shall present by explicitly contrasting them with those of Peters.

17

The central aspect of emotion for Peters is the appraisal, which is a special form of cognition or judgement in which the subject is affected by what he sees or otherwise apprehends. But it is as 'conceptual' as any neutral judgement. Objects are appraised *as* 'pleasing or displeasing, beneficial or harmful' in some mode or other. MacMurray entirely supports Peters's stress on the 'object-directedness' of emotion. Emotions, or feelings – MacMurray quite definitely uses these terms as synonyms, are not just sensations of the subject. They are essentially referred to something apprehended or perceived, necessarily directed to an object. But there is no emphasis on the conceptual nature of emotional apprehension for MacMurray. It is not a case of conceptual grasp 'with a feeling side' to it. 'In feeling emotions', he says, 'we feel the things to which the emotions refer' (1935a, p. 25). That is, we apprehend the object through feeling itself. The suggestion is that emotional apprehension is *pre*-conceptual. To this must be added another point. The proper objects of emotion are 'the value and significance of real things' (p. 31). It is the value aspects of objects that we feelingly apprehend. Although it could be argued that Peters really agrees with this, MacMurray has a more robust or 'objective' idea of value than Peters.

MacMurray strongly disagrees with Peters's attempt to drive a wedge between emotion and motive: 'all motives belong to our emotional life' (ibid., p. 13), 'our emotional life . . . alone contains the motives from which our conduct springs' (p. 49). It must be remembered, however, that Peters uses 'motive' in a somewhat technical way. Bereavement, for Peters, could not be a 'motive' for going into mourning, since expressive behaviour does not count as action for him, and talk of 'motive' is only in place when actions need to be explained, usually in terms of means to ends (1970, p. 177). And again, not all behaviour is accompanied by states of disturbance or upheaval in which things 'come over' people. However, we have given our reasons for thinking that there is 'passivity' in any kind of 'being affected' by things. This phenomenon is in fact at the heart of MacMurray's account, though is much underplayed by Peters. The former does not explicitly concern himself at all with the perturbations and upheavals, the loss of control, that Peters strongly emphasises. In terms of linguistic analysis Peters may be right here. To call a man 'emotional' *is* often to draw attention to very strong, perhaps overmastering, feeling: 'stop getting emotional' usually means 'control yourself' or 'don't let yourself be mastered by feeling'. On the other hand the simple noun 'emotion' *is* often used as synonymous with 'feeling'. But these linguistic points matter far less than the fact that feeling is the most pervasive characteristic of experience. We can perhaps sum up this brief discussion by saying that whereas Peters tends to concentrate on emotional disturbances or outbursts, MacMurray tends to concentrate on experiences of 'being affected', in which the value and significance of things come – possibly quite quietly – home to us. It is clear that if emotion is taken in *this* sense there must be a very close connection between it and 'motive' (understood quite generally as 'reason for action').

But the main value of MacMurray's treatment does not lie in any kind of analysis – conceptual or phenomenological – of emotion or feeling, but in its account of the relations between feeling, reason and thought, and the relative places these occupy, or should occupy, in human life. In much of this he differs profoundly from Peters, as the following schematic summary will make clear. It may be as well to point out in advance, however, that what Peters calls 'reason' MacMurray calls 'thought' or 'the intellectual life'.

(1) Man's Rational Nature

MacMurray links man's rationality to his nature as a responsible yet fallible person trusting in his own native powers and capacities to apprehend and respond to the world outside him. Peters links it to his nature as a social being, who internalises social rules and procedures which provide him with guarantees against failure in his approach to things.

MacMurray's position here is very closely allied to that of Polanyi. He stresses that it is a task of education to bring children to the position where they can *trust* their own powers to grasp the nature of reality. Polanyi emphasises that every action of a living being, including a rational person, involves commitment, or reliance on powers or principles that he cannot fully comprehend. Perception, feeling and thought are all ways of grasping reality, or aspects of reality. We have these powers as the living beings we are, and have to learn to rely on them in spite of the social pressures that tempt the individual towards irrational reliance on others (though Polanyi, unlike MacMurray, gives full weight to the need to rely on *traditions* of thought and feeling). Having to rely on our own powers does make us vulnerable to error, but if we react properly to mistakes we will naturally learn from them. Trust in life is essential.

Against this Peters stresses man's social nature, his need to be taught the rules and procedures that enable him to be rational, and the testing procedures that 'guarantee objectivity and the escape from arbitrariness'. We have already commented on this. But we may well here in addition recall a favourite theme of Max Scheler's: the general fear and mistrust of life characteristic of philosophies that stress 'criteria'. This is no stronger in Peters than in most English postwar philosophers but, on the other hand, it is no weaker either.

(2) The Nature of Reason

MacMurray primarily characterises reason as the capacity to respond to the world as it is in itself; its most fundamental aspect is emotional reason, which is the capacity to respond through the use of the senses to the objective values the world contains. The biggest obstacles to a rational life are a predominantly instrumental, and the closely allied intellectual, approaches to things. For Peters, reason is first and foremost the use of public rules and procedures, which enable one to make sense of the world and find one's way in it. Analysis, means-ends thinking and the scientific approach are central features of reason, and the chief obstacle to rationality is emotion.

MacMurray's idea of reason as a response to the nature of the world as it is in itself might seem to be in the end no different from the concern that clearly underlies Peters's stress on the need to incorporate social rules and procedures. For the presupposition here is that a human being does not really have any 'experience', in the sense of 'ordered' or 'intelligible' experience, unless he possesses and makes use of some ordering device. But the only means we have are the conceptual schemes (interpreted as rules for ordering experience) of language, which is indubitably a social possession. Thus, according to Hirst and Peters, one *cannot* respond to the nature of the world as it is in itself except by employing the rules and procedures that underlie human languages (Hirst and Peters, 1970, p. 62). They imply that pre-conceptual experience is a succession of meaningless sensations; learning language is like putting on a pair of spectacles that transforms this chaos into an ordered whole.

MacMurray does not explicitly discuss this question, but it is clear what sort of things he might say in reply. To approach life in the way described by Hirst and Peters is to make it impossible to apprehend the world in new and unexpected ways. It is to *force* the world to conform to one's preconceptions about it. And because concepts are products of thought, and the main characteristic of thinking is its instrumentality, these preconceptions do not even arise from our intimate selves, but from a more superficial layer of the self. A conceptual apparatus thus *prevents* us from responding to the world as it is in itself.

They might reply that this is impossible. If experience is nothing without concepts, then we might as well cease to worry about pre-conceptual experience altogether. But suppose it could be shown that pre-conceptual experience was feeling, and that feeling had a structure of its own that was independent of, but essential for, the 'conceptual structures' provided by language? This is clearly something like MacMurray's assumption, and the position that will be more fully investigated below. It must suffice here to have pointed to the real difference between MacMurray and Peters. For the former 'the world as it is in itself' can be *felt*, can be grasped emotionally. For the latter this is impossible: there can be no significant experience that does not depend on the conceptual apparatus and other rules of language.

It is clear now why MacMurray regards the rationality of emotion as more fundamental than the rationality of thought. Things cannot be rightly or correctly thought unless they are rightly or correctly felt, because thought is at one remove from its object. Thus rational thought must rest on rational feeling, because only on this assumption is thinking really responsive to the nature of reality.

It should be clear now too why MacMurray constantly stresses the use of the senses. The senses are our gateway to reality. Unless we 'live' in our senses as opposed to our thoughts, unless we constantly keep our eyes and ears open instead of using them merely as adjuncts to thinking, which necessarily entails missing a great deal, we cannot properly 'feel' reality and, in particular, the values the world contains (its beauty, goodness and significance). The instrumental and intellectual approaches to things both hinder this: in the former we take in the reality of things only to the extent that we can use it to solve our practical problems; in the latter we take it in only if it matches some 'theory' or 'conceptual scheme' we are working with or trying to promote. Both these approaches are in the end self-centred rather than world-centred or rational.

(3) The Relation of Thought and Feeling

Rational thought, according to MacMurray, depends on rational feeling, on feeling which enables its own principles of order to take effect. Peters holds that rational feeling depends on rational thought, which means that feeling has to be disciplined by authority as the guardian of social rules and procedures.

It would be useful to insert at this point two passages in which MacMurray deals with this question (1935a, pp. 26, 75):

It is not that our feelings have a secondary and subordinate capacity for being rational or irrational. It is that reason is primarily an affair of emotion, and that the rationality of thought is the derivative and secondary one. For if reason is the capacity to *act* in terms of the nature of the object, it is emotion which stands directly behind activity determining its substance and direction, while thought is related to action indirectly and through emotion, determining only its form, and that only partially.

The emotional life is not simply a part or an aspect of human life
. . . It is the core and essence of human life. The intellect arises
out of it, is rooted in it, draws its nourishment and sustenance from
it, and is the subordinate partner in the human economy. This is
because the intellect is essentially instrumental.

The first passage reminds us that 'reason' is not something in itself.
It is men and women who are rational and irrational, and they show
this in what they *do*. Thinking is a kind of behaviour, and thus again
thought can only be rational or irrational if it is actually being thought
by a thinker. But all human behaviour, including thinking, has to be
'motivated', and because motives are bound up inextricably with
emotions, emotions must be primary. MacMurray is not just anticipating
Peters's observation that the rational life is impossible without the
rational passions. Peters, as we have seen, insists that there are criteria
of rationality *not* derived from feeling. MacMurray's point is that even
in a simple syllogism one has to 'move' from premisses to conclusion.
In the light of the data that Socrates is a man and all men are mortal
one *draws* the conclusion that Socrates is mortal. That is, one does
something. It is ultimately *feeling* that licenses the inference, in the sense
that only if one feels the step to be right does one allow oneself to make
the ultimate mental move, and only if this feeling is a rational feeling
is one rationally motivated to make it. Of course, one may claim that
one is 'following the rules of inference'. But one has to respect them,
to have some positive feeling for them, to feel that they are genuine guides
to rationality. All appeal to rules is thus respect for 'traditional feeling'
rather than one's own feeling.

The second passage quoted above clearly expresses the main theme
of MacMurray's treatment of emotion. The emotional life of feeling 'is
the core and essence of human life'. We all instinctively acknowledge
this. For it is in our emotional lives that we are in direct contact with
reality itself. The intellect, which operates with concepts, is rooted in
it both in that concepts must, if they are to be rational, be formed from
the raw material of what is feelingly apprehended, and also in that the
operations of conceptual thought need to be motivated, by feeling and
emotion, and checked with reference to our feelings of appropriateness,
inappropriateness, and so on. Again, its *ends* must be derived from
emotion. Even if the end of our thinking is the apprehension of reality,
our *sense* of reality has to be a feeling-apprehension, because only in
feeling are we directly in touch with reality.

How, then, can we trust our feelings and know that they are a sure
guide to reality? Obviously they are not infallible. Would it not be wiser
to trust to 'principles of reason', coolly and calmly elaborated and handed
on in social rules and precepts from which all trace of emotion and

feeling has been drained? The appeal to 'social rules' has already been discussed. Social rules must come from somewhere and the only plausible origin is individual thinkers. So how can we tell that feeling is reliable? In practice we simply *have* to rely on it. And it makes perfect sense to talk of learning by experience, as MacMurray does, even if we cannot completely elucidate the meaning of this phrase. Life itself does seem to teach us, sometimes admittedly very slowly, when we can trust our feelings and when we cannot. But given that these things happen, and given that those who trust in the intellect often seem thoroughly disordered in their feelings, it seems as though there must be some principle of order in feeling itself. The truly rational man, for MacMurray, teaches himself to sense the structure of feeling in himself, to 'listen' to his feelings, and to regulate his life accordingly. He is careful to maintain a harmony between thought and emotion, never letting the former over-rule the latter. He makes sure that his feeling really is directed *outwards,* towards the 'not-self'. 'In general, we may say that excitement is a good test of the unreality of feeling. When anything excites us and stimulates feelings in us, we are not feeling *it*' (1935b, p. 152). Thus it is always a danger sign when someone starts to enjoy his feelings. All this makes sense if feeling is more central to man, intellect more peripheral. In listening out for the structure of one's feeling, one is discovering what one really wants and what one really believes – indeed, one is discovering who one is. 'Know thyself', said Socrates. This turns out to mean, according to MacMurray, 'discover the structure of feeling and emotion (and hence motive) within yourself and live accordingly'.

(4)   The Relation of Action and Feeling

For MacMurray the ideal action is the spontaneous expression of feeling, since such actions keep us in touch with the living heart of ourselves and give us the sense of being most fully alive. If thought intervenes we lose our personal wholeness. For Peters the ideal action is reasoned and considered in the light of moral and prudential criteria. Although the rational passions may be necessary, feeling and emotion in general are always to be kept out, or at least regarded with considerable suspicion, since they are almost invariably disruptive.

To common sense there seems something heavy-handed about Peters's ideal. Is deliberation or reasoning 'in the full sense' *really* necessary for rational action, we may ask. If one presses this point to 'rationalist' or 'intellectualist' philosophers who see things like Peters, they tend to retreat. There must be 'something like' deliberation, but it need not take a long time. Reasons must have been consulted at some time, and must always be 'operative' in a person's behaviour, but do not actually have to be 'consulted' or 'applied' at the moment of action. And so on. One begins to wonder, in fact, whether Peters's description of 'emotional reactions' does not come near to fitting both what MacMurray praises and what 'rationalist' philosophers can be induced to retreat towards. It was characteristic of these that one's appraisal of the situation was 'intuitive' or 'subliminal'; there was no explicit means-ends thinking involved, 'no consideration of possible ends of action'. Peters's examples – lashing out in anger or starting with fear – seem beside the point. What about holding a shop door open to let a heavily laden customer out before entering oneself, gradually applying the brakes because one senses that the car in front is going to turn right (though it has not signalled), smiling at one's neighbour in the audience when the speaker has just made a good joke, amplifying a point in a lesson when a pupil momentarily betrays incomprehension? These are absolutely typical of the actions of ordinary life. They are not habitual in a mechanical sense, but are essentially responses to individual situations that may never have occurred to one before in quite the same form. Thus they could not be entirely based on rules and principles, though the existence of sentiments or tendencies to be, perhaps, considerate, cautious or prudent, sociable and adaptable are likely to underlie them. They are (or may be) rational in MacMurray's sense, in that they are responses to things as they are, being compounded of cognition, feeling and conation (or impulse), since there is an apprehension of 'fact' and of value and a responding impulse, accompanied by feeling, to act in certain ways.

MacMurray, of course, does not deny that deliberation is sometimes appropriate, just as he admits that the instrumental action often is (though he does overdo his opposition). His main concern is to get us to see that spontaneous responses to situations, based largely on feeling and what Peters calls 'low-level' cognition, are just as rational, indeed, in many cases *more* rational, than actions in which thought intervenes between feeling-impulse and act. For the situations of ordinary life are constantly changing, and in a great many cases only the immediate response will do justice to them.

What is more, failure to act spontaneously from feeling (that is, wholeheartedly) in response to the nature of the situation brings about a loss of personal wholeness. This is a favourite theme of MacMurray's. The intellect, he says, because it uses concepts, 'must divide and . . . abstract. It is in the emotional life that the unity of personality . . . is realized and maintained' (1935a, p. 77). The intellect goes in for specialisation and narrowness. Hence the chaos of competing claims, interests, factions, and so on, in our 'intellectualist' society. Spontaneous action binds our 'inner' and our 'outer' sides together, binds us to the people we are dealing with, gives us a sense of being part of a whole.

24

Deliberation and reasoning, however necessary in certain areas of life, detach and withdraw us from ourselves, from others and the world, and if they are emphasised unduly lead to a sense of futility and meaninglessness. The effect of Peters's analysis, by contrast, is to suggest that the intellect is the heart of the person, since rationality is a matter of the correct application of concepts and rules. For MacMurray such recommendations (however qualified they may be here and there) are a recipe for despair.

We must add to this account of MacMurray's differences from Peters a few more points. I mentioned above that MacMurray's idea of value is rather more robust and objective than Peters's. His notion of 'responding to reality' is not simply the idea that, given that we have certain needs or wants, we have to take account of the nature of reality if we would be successful. Rather, it is part of our nature as rational beings to 'conform' to reality in the sense of letting it dictate to us what we should feel and what we should do (just as we think we should let it dictate to us what we should believe). For values – with the 'demands' that are part of our experience of them – are 'in' the world, objective features or aspects of it. This is a different view from Peters's. For him the ultimate source of imperatives (or 'demands') is not the world itself but the 'logic' of moral discourse. He tries to show that certain moral principles, from which all other important moral principles can be derived, are 'presupposed' in the rational activity of asking the question 'what ought I to do?' (1966, pp. 114–16). This is an attempt to derive ultimate value from 'logic' or reasoning itself. Since, for him, there is no such thing as a 'world' that can *be* 'directly experienced', the source of moral demands must be the next best thing: the rules and procedures of public reason.

MacMurray puts a great deal of stress on art and religion in his account of rational feeling. One of his main arguments in favour of the existence of this is as follows. Given that man is by nature a rational being, that art and religion are 'characteristic and essential expression[s] of human nature' (1935a, p. 19), and that art and religion are closely bound up with feeling and emotion, there must be an emotional as well as an intellectual expression of reason. Science, by contrast, is essentially intellectual and conceptual, and can only give an 'instrumental' account of things. This is because conceptualising is the singling out of general features that are easy to identify and can be used as the basis of experiments, and so on. Thus a person whose education is largely scientific is in danger of being cut off from the real world; he will see everything under some concept that has proved useful in some respect. Hence MacMurray's plea for art and religion as necessary counterpoises. These, because of their basis in feeling, keep the individual in touch

25

with the world and himself and prevent the slide into instrumentalism, and the obsession with power and control, that science encourages. We should note here that MacMurray's stress on the need for religion is very far from being a piece of orthodox Christian evangelism, and he denies that any actual religion has yet realised the essential religious goal of community. Art, by contrast, is 'essentially individual and contemplative', representing 'the effort to become aware of the significance of individuals in themselves through an emotional apprehension of them' (ibid., p. 60).

As a final aid to the comprehensive grasp of MacMurray's position we shall sketch out in summary fashion his ideas on the *education* of the emotions. The fundamental aspect of this is the training of the individual's sensibility. This means he is encouraged to live in and savour life through the senses, so that he can apprehend the true nature of things in themselves, especially their value, both positive and negative. In this way the centre of gravity of feeling is shifted from the self to the world outside, and it becomes possible to grasp reality as a whole. Individuals come to trust in their own power to grasp reality for themselves. The process achieves its goal once the individual's responses to the world are rational or objective, that is, are what the situation calls for, whether or not this response is pleasant or useful. Education of the emotions also involves encouraging and refining forms of activity which are spontaneous expressions in action of rational emotion. Thus the individual is enabled to act with the whole of himself, spontaneously, non-mechanically and freely, and he is in close touch with the sources of vitality in human life.

The main ways of achieving emotional education are through art and religion, by encouraging children to live in the senses for the joy of it, by not suppressing their sensitivity to the world (especially to its negative side), by letting them learn through the discipline of life and experience itself, and *not* by exploiting their natural affection and reverence for authority.

Critique of John MacMurray's Views

In interpreting MacMurray's writings on feeling and emotion we must not forget his polemical intent. He wanted above all to 'free feeling', just as thought had been freed during the seventeenth century and earlier to make possible the rise and triumph of science and technology, and to reinstate the idea of rational feeling (cf. Lewis, 1978, pp. 14ff.). These practical concerns lead him into an exaggerated rejection of the instrumental approach to the world. The fact is that we have to adopt this attitude to stay alive. Without it we would not be able to afford to enjoy the life of the senses and respond to the nature of the world as it is in itself. There is also his exaggerated mistrust of thought. But instrumental thought is not the only kind of thought. Thought serves technique, certainly, but it also serves our search for meaning and significance, as much of MacMurray's own philosophical work implicitly demonstrates.

A related point concerns his stress on the need to direct the life of feeling away from the self. The life of 'getting and spending' is certainly egocentric, since it involves approaching the world simply as source of means to attain our ends – ends being derived directly from the self, in the form of needs or wants. Education of feeling involves getting the individual to respond to the values of the world as they are in themselves, to admire beauty and goodness and shun ugliness and evil not because *we* like, want, or need these things (and wish to be rid of their negative counterparts) but 'for their own sakes', or perhaps as an expression of our oneness with the world. But it might well be argued that just as enjoyment of and response to the world as it is in itself depend in fact on our also taking up an instrumental attitude towards it, so other-directed feelings depend somehow on self-directed feelings. You cannot love others until you love yourself; you cannot love God until you love others. The educational problems would thus not be a matter of replacing one lot of feelings by another but of ensuring a proper balance between them.

MacMurray is also open to the charge of putting too much emphasis on pre-conceptual knowing, on feeling-awareness, which is fleeting, uncertain, wavering and often dim. Surely we *need* to use concepts in order to know properly (that is, surely, confidently, firmly and clearly) – *a fortiori* if we are to *communicate* what we know with any precision (though perhaps if we are artists we need not), and certainly whenever we wish to generalise. MacMurray is certainly right in his assumption of the importance of pre-conceptual knowing. It is absolutely essential in some spheres of knowledge. For instance, someone asks me what a person I have just met is like. How am I to answer? Clearly I have to recall and re-live my feeling-experience of the person, go back in feeling to the moment of genuine encounter, when the reality of the person impinged on me. It may, of course, be too late. The experience may be beyond recall. But, unless it was particularly striking (we must surely all possess *some* memories of people, places and experiences that are almost entirely made up of the 'feeling-flavour' they left behind), it will need to be fleshed forth in concepts if I am to continue to remember it. Indeed, once we find ourselves reflecting on our experiences we normally proceed to conceptualise their objects unprompted by others. For there is a sense in which the knowledge is still not yet accessible to the whole of ourselves if it remains pre-conceptual. Nevertheless, it is to my mind absurd to claim that it is 'nothing' before we clothe it in concepts. Indeed, we may often be well aware that we cannot find concepts to do justice to what we have pre-conceptually known (and still retain in perhaps gradually fading form); the pre-conceptual cognition, with its relative weakness and impermanence, may not be a genuine 'grasp' but it *is* an 'impression' – indeed, it may be a deep and lasting impression – and it is quite distinct from the conceptual 'clothing' with which we may or may not succeed in adequately 'fixing' it.

It seems to me that MacMurray does not give sufficient attention to these considerations. He fails to convey to us a coherent picture of human being into which pre-conceptual awareness and conceptual knowledge, feeling and thought, self-related and world-related feelings, egocentricity and world-openness can be convincingly fitted. In spite of his valuable emphasis on the centrality of feeling for human life, vitality and 'wholeness', his picture of the person remains vague.

This becomes even clearer when we consider his almost exclusive stress on individuality in feeling. The individual person must be encouraged to feel for himself, or his feelings will be second-hand, unreal, 'traditional'. Faced with a certain grey uniformity of feeling in the persons we encounter, of sentimentality and slavish following of 'feeling-fashion', one may perhaps be excused for an exaggerated stress on the individual. There is a sense, too, in which feeling *must* be individual once the question of its rationality has been raised in the person's mind. Even if I decide to follow some tradition of feeling, it is still I who have to feel that this tradition is the right one for me to follow. But, however much we may agree with MacMurray that reason is not primarily social, a great deal of human *life* is social. To be born into a community and to learn its language is, willy-nilly, to be initiated into a tradition of feeling. One of the most effective ways of extending the range of one's feelings is to entrust oneself to new communities, to learn their 'languages' with their own traditions of feeling. It is, of course, always possible that individuals will merely go through the motions of feeling like their new fellows, of copying their forms of expression, and so on. It is clearly vital that this stage is left behind. But it is plausible to suggest that this *is* a necessary step, for all but a handful of highly exceptional individuals, in the development of the emotional life. Neither in the spheres of conceptual knowledge nor in those of pre-conceptual feeling-awareness can the majority of us 'go it alone'. We are social beings and, although our personal life is in the end higher or deeper than our social life, we need to *base* it on communal life. In this too, then, MacMurray seems to aim straight for the 'higher', ignoring the need for foundations.

Another problem of MacMurray's account concerns his *analysis* of feeling or emotion. This, it must be said, is largely implicit. But it seems to cover more than one sort of thing. On the one hand it is in emotion or feeling that we grasp the values the world contains; we *feel* the beauty of a cloudy sky, the goodness of an act of alms-giving. In such 'acts' of apprehension we let the value of things 'speak' to us. This is the phenomenon of 'being affected'. On the other hand, *motives* are emotional too. MacMurray may mean that our 'being affected' calls forth a responsive impulse in us − to stop what we are doing and gaze at the cloudscape, to perform some generous act ourselves. But the experience of impulse, of feeling a prompting or a desire to *do* something, is surely a different sort of phenomenon. In 'being affected' the direction of 'movement' is from the object to us; in feeling an impulse or tendency the direction is reversed, and goes outwards from us to the world. Certainly the two go essentially together, but they are not the same. What is more, we may experience feelings of impulse or desire which are not in the first instance responses to objects apprehended, but which seem to come directly from within us. For example, we may feel lonely. This may be sparked off by the sight of groups of friends, but our feelings are not responses to these objects. They rather betray a lack, a need, and a desire to fill it. These feelings come from within. But then again our impulse to gaze at the beauties of the sky, or emulate the generosity of the alms-giver, is distinct from our responses of wondering delight at the beauty or admiration at the act. These things are indeed closely bound up together. It is possible that they merely represent 'points of emphasis' of experience that is lived as undivided. But for the purpose of philosophical analysis it is important to make these distinctions. There is the feeling-experience of value, the response in feeling and the experience of impulse. All are 'emotional' in that they are part of our affective lives. An adequate philosophical account of emotion must make room for all three, and not forget in addition the experience of surrender of agency in the face of feelings that have become too much for us.

One final point concerns MacMurray's conception of value, and the notion of feeling and acting as the situation requires. The question may arise in the reader's mind: can one ever be *purely* responsive to the world? Is it really conceivable that a man should simply 'respond' to things as they are, even though he has no interest of his own and no purpose to achieve in doing so? But 'the world' contains other people, and moral experience quite unequivocally forbids our regarding others merely instrumentally. It must suffice here to say that MacMurray does not address himself to the problem this raises, which demands solution in terms of a comprehensive picture of human nature. One aspect of this would be an analysis of our experience of value. When MacMurray talks of our acting as the situation requires, this is no more than is in fact 'given' in value-experience. Every experience of value contains as a component an experience of being 'demanded', 'required', 'challenged', 'invited', or otherwise 'solicited' to react in some way or other, and this solicitation is experienced as somehow emerging from the situation.

These 'demands' and so on are thus, in a real sense, items in the world, since we experience them as 'part of' the situation confronting us. They are 'felt' as part of the total value-experiences that give rise to them.

If someone asks for a 'justification' of these demands then various courses are open to us. We may insist that they are self-justifying. Many people find no difficulty in this answer; the experiences are such that no question of justification arises for them – and we may add that this can be so whether or not the individual in question *conforms* to the demand. Alternatively we may try to link obedience to demands to something the individual already regards as important for him (self-respect, social respectability or harmony, 'respect for persons', etc.). But if these attempts fail and it is insisted that some philosophical justification be found, then we have, I am sure, to return to the question of human nature and the attempt to find a solution in a comprehensive picture of what human being is.

It seems to me that the germs of a solution are to be found in MacMurray's hints of a structure of feeling which orders the life of feeling and makes it rational. We must be able to conceive of value – value in itself, that is – as somehow the implicit goal of human striving; being affected by such value is then the satisfied finding of what one was seeking. This picture will be incomplete unless we also account for the fact that people frequently appear to be indifferent to value-in-itself and prefer to concentrate on self-related values. But these matters will be taken up more fully below.

3

General Survey of the Affective Sphere

After this fairly detailed survey and discussion of the contribution to our theme of Peters and MacMurray, which has served to open up the subject, I turn to a more general treatment of feeling and emotion. For the reasons given above, this is only possible within severe limits. For the very phenomena of emotion and feeling are elusive. It is not only that an extreme looseness of linguistic usage obtains in the field; the very field itself seems to be in doubt. But it may nevertheless prove instructive to pose certain general questions and see how they have been answered in the main literature available. In keeping with the central intention of this book, my main sources are philosophical; but I have also consulted psychological works.

Demarcating the Affective Sphere of Experience

I have chosen to talk mainly about 'the Affective' rather than about 'feeling' or 'emotion' because, although the last two terms are also used by some writers in the highly general way I here intend, more writers use them, especially 'emotion', to denote *part* of the field than the term 'the Affective' (or 'the affective sphere', etc.). It thus seems more appropriate to regard 'emotion' and 'feeling' primarily as marking off *aspects* of the 'affective sphere', rather than denoting the sphere itself. However I shall not stick rigidly to this usage.

(1) Is There a Principle of Unity?

One cannot easily make a general survey of answers to this question since not many authors seem to be addressing themselves to it and very few explicitly separate it from their attempts to answer questions like

31

'what is feeling?' or 'what is emotion?' – where they may or may not be regarding 'feeling' and 'emotion' as names of items within the larger field that I have labelled 'the Affective'.

James Hillman stresses, as I have done, the enormous extent of disagreement about the answer to this question (1960). Another eloquent witness to this state of affairs is the French psychologist E. Claparède, who states: 'the psychology of affective processes is the most confused chapter in all psychology'. Psychologists, he goes on, 'are in agreement neither on the facts nor on the words' (1928, p. 157). This disagreement is such that some psychologists have come to deny that the Affective (or 'emotion') refers to anything specific at all (Hillman, 1960, pp. 36f.). E. Duffy, another psychologist, concludes that affective phenomena can only be demarcated from other psychic phenomena with reference to a change of energy level (1941, p. 131). But a few thinkers do give answers to this general question.

William James implies that affective experience is experience involving 'the bodily sounding-board' (1884, pp. 31ff.). This is a theme we have not so far paid much attention to, but which will occupy us more fully in a few pages' time.

G. H. Bantock points out that the idea of movement is fundamental to the etymology of 'emotion' (taken in the most general sense) and implies (like Duffy) that it is 'something which involves alterations – however slight – to a person's psychic equilibrium, with possible repercussions on conduct' (1967, p. 65). Such emphasis on the dynamic aspects of affectivity reinforces the idea that emotion and motive are intimately connected.

Several authors, including those who have provided the most comprehensive and wide-ranging accounts of the Affective, characterise it experientially. Hillman notes that the rejection of affective phenomena is especially characteristic of psychologists who deny any reality to the inner life. This suggests, he says, 'that emotion and psychic reality have some significant relation' (1960, pp. 36f.). Susanne Langer defines feeling as 'the mark of mentality' (1967, Vol. I, p. 4), and Louis Arnaud Reid calls it 'the inner side of conscious experience' (1976–7, p. 168).

On the other hand, Klages (1950, p. 125), Hillman, Lersch (1954) and Strasser (1977, p. 92) characterise it as the most intimate *form* of experience, though Strasser, in particular, argues that mental acts undergo a process of development from the most intimate to the most superficial layer of the person, which entails that all experience must at least originate in affectivity.

Lersch, with his observation that the objects of affective experience are not given *as* objects but pre-conceptually, also specifically relates the characterisation of the Affective to the idea of levels within the person (1954, pp. 302–4).

(2) How Are the Affective and the Conative Distinguished?

Psychologists in the United Kingdom have traditionally started out with the assumption that there are three spheres of psychic experience or activity: the Affective, the Conative and the Cognitive. The Cognitive (to do with 'knowledge') is usually taken to comprise all kinds of perception, both inner and outer, memory, imagination and all kinds of thinking and reasoning. Conation comprises impulse, desire, wishing and willing. We have already begun to engage in the question of how affection and conation are related in our treatment of the emotion-motive question above. Ordinary experience suggests that the relation is very close. One must, of course, point out once more when citing the support of this or that author for this or that view that the exact range of phenomena intended to be covered by the terms I have taken to denote the Affective is not always, if ever, clear.

But a large number of writers take it for granted that there is a very close connection between the Affective and conation. These include psychologists (Shand, McDougall, Dumas, Leeper – all in Arnold, 1968 – and M. Phillips, 1937), the philosopher-psychologist Lersch, and various philosophers (including Bergson, Findlay, Brentano, Hillman, Melden, Pitcher, Reiner, Stein, Scheler and Strasser). Leeper (1948, p. 188) and Arnold and Gasson (1954, p. 203) seem to deny that there is any distinction between affection and conation at all. Lersch, while continuing to regard them as separable to some degree, as they surely are, makes impulse a component of feeling, feeling arise from impulse, and, more important, argues that the structure of 'movements of feeling' (roughly, experiences of 'being affected') parallels the structure of impulse.

On the other hand, some writers deny the close connection, though they in fact discuss aspects of the Affective rather than the sphere as such (for the somewhat exceptional views of Peters see above, pp. 13f). G. Dumas, for instance, argues that in emotion proper (the phenomenon of surrender of agency sketched above) there is no tendency towards a goal. A man who simply feels afraid will flee, or seek means of flight; one who suffers the *emotion* of fear is petrified and stays rooted to the spot, no longer having either command of his limbs or even the ability to discern what he needs to do (1948, p. 113). M. Pradines argues that no impulses, tendencies, and so on, are closely connected to sentiments, since these long-term regulators of behaviour are operative independent of circumstances (1958, p. 191). Sentiments will occupy us below, but it may be said here that in so far as they are not felt sentiments should not be classified as purely affective phenomena at all, since they connote thought and choice. Then, again, G. D. Marshall writes: 'in being affected we do not necessarily acquire a spring of action' (1968, p. 247). Like Peters, he cites 'depressive affections'. What is not clear here is whether he has in mind depressive *moods*, which have a different sort of relation to conative and other affective phenomena, to be discussed below, or depressive *feelings* (grieving at, being sad about, etc.). The latter do seem to issue in conations towards inactivity, sources of comfort, avoidance of society, and so on, as I suggested above. But moods raise special problems of their own. It remains true that the vast majority of writers either explicitly state, or imply, a very close connection between affectivity and conation. This is clearly not a strictly 'conceptual' or 'logical' connection, and certainly admits of exceptions. But in the 'economy' of human life they must in general go together. The connection is not just contingent, as though they equally well might not. It is in some sense necessary and intelligible that they do.

If this is so, then we should expect most affective experiences to be analysable at least in part in terms of impulse or tendency; contrariwise, experiences of being impelled or driven, of psychic want or lack, to be at least in part analysable in terms of feeling (in a broad sense). It seems to me that one wants both to accept this and to reject it. For purposes of analysis surely the two are distinct: the *concept* of being affected does not itself contain the idea of impulse, and vice versa. But it is hardly plausible to maintain this of *experience* (see also pp. 29f above). These considerations lead one back to a dynamic conception of mind rather than a static one and to some acceptance of psychic levels. This will become clearer when we have looked at the next section.

(3) How Are the Affective and the Cognitive Related?

The widespread view that affective phenomena tend to interfere with all sorts of cognition (though they prepare the way for it via 'interest', 'curiosity', or the like; e.g. Bantock, 1967, pp. 69f.) presupposes their separateness. Nevertheless, Leeper says that emotional processes 'ought to be seen as one type of perceptual process' (1963, p. 243), Descartes characterised passion as unclear thought, and Whitehead (reported in Hillman, 1960, p. 193) regarded it as the 'primary mode of cognition'. We have seen, too, that MacMurray holds that in emotion we 'feel' objects and that Peters calls emotion a 'type of cognition', though only a 'low-level' one because of the element of passivity involved (Aschenbrenner, however, makes a firm separation between 'appraisals which help condition hope and fear' and 'hope and fear themselves'; 1971, p. 55). Findlay endorses Meinong's view that emotion has a 'presentative function'; it is in feeling and desire that values are brought home to us (Findlay, 1963, p. 304). Reid argues that in our knowledge of other persons, 'If there is an absence of cognitive feeling, there is a lack of something in the knowing' (1976–7, p. 175).

Other writers speak of a kind of 'foreknowledge' or 'pre-cognition' in feeling. Harold Osborne discusses the difficulty of describing unusual perceptual qualities without using the language of feeling (1963, p. 47):

> Only as they become more familiar, or clearer to cognition, the feeling fades and the quality which was first intimated through feeling is later apprehended without affective tone in a more penetrating and lucid perceptual act. Feeling seems as it were to grope ahead of perception and to put out cognitive tentacles in advance of clear apprehension.

Compare this passage from Edith Stein (1970, pp. 97f.):

> Knowledge not yet realised is felt as a value. This feeling of value is the source of all cognitive striving . . . An object proffers itself to me as dark, veiled, and unclear. It stands there as something which demands exposure and clarification.

Arnold and Gasson talk of emotions 'aim[ing] at the possession of suitable objects' (1954, p. 212). Langer endorses Woodworth's view that drives (we would say 'impulses') are 'selective as well as motivating' (1967, Vol. I, p. 289). Lersch says that every experience of need is also an anticipation, a 'prehension' (*Vorgriff*) of the future. If the Affective and the Conative can be regarded as essentially involving each other we have to understand them as though they already somehow 'knew' what they were looking for, or what would satisfy them. This phenomenon, which we prefer to see in dynamic or developmental terms, is frequently interpreted in 'logical' ones, and in the works of Peters, Findlay and others becomes the idea that one can logically only be proud of what is of value and connected to oneself, or angry with something that has 'crossed' one, and so forth.

(4) What Is the Relation between Feeling and Thought?

We can only make satisfactory sense of many of the opinions and observations of the thinkers recorded here if we take the idea of psychic levels, or of stratification, seriously. The reason for the differences of opinion as to whether affection and conation, affection and cognition, and then again conation and cognition are or are not distinct is that at one level of the mind they are and at another they are not. Conceptually speaking, that is, at the level of conceptual thinking, there is a distinction;

pre-conceptually, at the level of impulse and feeling-awareness (of direct experience), there is not. Hence Lersch can say that cognition, affection and conation are not only present in all experience but cannot really be disentangled; picking out one or the other is merely the acknowledgement of a certain prominence or emphasis in experience. 'Hence the formation of psychological concepts is much more a matter of accentuating than of demarcating', though we may add that once the concepts *have* been formed, we naturally tend to assume that they mark clear distinctions under all circumstances.

Thus (see section (2) above), to the extent that the existence of sentiments implies that their subject has *thought about* what he really wants and values, we are not now surprised to find it claimed that sentiments do not imply conation. The very fact that they can be 'operative independent of circumstances' shows us that they have attained the kind of 'logical' or 'ideal', and hence steady and clear, existence that conceptual thinking bestows on its objects; this could never be true of experienced feelings. We can see now, too, why Descartes called passion 'unclear thought'; he is talking of pre-conceptual, and hence fleeting, unsteady and clouded awareness, which is inseparable from feeling and conation (cf. the quotation from Edith Stein above).

We can now also make sense of Whitehead's claim that emotion is the 'primary mode of cognition'. In this light we can understand Aschenbrenner's assertion that the existence of 'moral affects' (indignation, resentment, shame, penitence, remorse, and so on) is 'a material or formal condition' for that of moral judgements (1971, p. 104), and Langer's claim that the 'feelings' of 'symbolic activity' ('strain and expectation, vagueness and clearness, ease and frustration, and the very interesting "sense of rightness" that closes a finished thought process') are 'really the ultimate criteria whereby we judge the validity of logical relations' (1967, Vol. I, p. 147). The idea is also supported by Claparède, who approvingly cites William James to this effect (1928, pp. 167ff.). It should be apparent now, also, why Hans Reiner says that willing has much less feeling-content than striving or impulse, which is heavily bound up with feeling. Though impulses somehow dimly 'point' towards the objects that will properly satisfy them, we can only fully know this by thinking about it. But in so far as we do, we rise above the level at which impulses could spontaneously convert themselves into action. Because thought has intervened an act of will (of conscious 'consent' to the striving) is required, and the decision can be taken relatively dispassionately (in the absence of experienced feeling) (Reiner, 1974, pp. 132f.). Findlay's interesting discussion of the distinction between 'warm' and 'cool' wanting is relevant here and, again, most easily understood in terms of stratification (1961, pp. 179ff.). We shall give this idea a fuller justification below.

(5) What Is the Place of the Body?

William James, as we have already observed, argued that it was primarily bodily involvement that distinguished feeling from judgement, a point also emphasised by, for example, Arnold and Gasson (1954, p. 203). We might now put this in our own terms by saying that experience at the level of feeling-awareness is more body-bound than that at the level of thought, which strives to become 'impersonal' – detached from the material person who happens to be thinking. As Edith Stein puts it: 'In "theoretical acts", such as acts of perception, imagination, relating or concluding, thinking, etc., I am turned to an object in such a way that the "I" and the acts are not there at all' (1970, p. 89).

Findlay, relating the idea more explicitly to our theme, argues that 'the tendency of emotional wants to have an unpractical expression in the inner economy of the body' is *a priori* intelligible, since this kind of expression is 'the least practical, the least object-bound' (1961, p. 168). Non-emotional or 'cool' wants, by contrast, strive for the detachment of thought, and practical expression in language. This line of thinking is clearly linked with Descartes' association of the bodily aspects of passion with what he called our passivity with regard to them. The implication here is that the real 'we', or the most important part of the self, is merely *subject* to the Affective. An extreme expression of the idea that there is a split between the real self and the bodily aspect of emotion is that of Sartre. He put forward the view that the bodily phenomena of emotion were 'used' by the self 'as a means of incantation', in order to cope with a situation that had become practically unmanageable (1948, p. 70).

Other writers, for example Marshall, remind us that the 'logical' subjects of affects are *persons*, not mere minds or bodies (1968, p. 245). The child psychologist K. M. B. Bridges also rejected the view, common in her day, that emotions were 'visceral pattern reactions' in favour of the idea that they were 'changes in the behaviour of the total personality' (1931, p. 198). We may recall here, too, MacMurray's insistence on the link between feeling and personal wholeness, a point also stressed by Hillman.

This emphasis on totality gains support from a consideration of the *sort* of bodily reactions involved in affective states and behaviour. It was once the hope of experimental psychologists and others that each particular emotion could be shown to have its own peculiar bodily manifestation, such that psychologists could come to use bodily symptoms as criteria of the emotions their subjects were experiencing. It is now generally realised that this is a hopeless undertaking. It is not only that certain emotions often show different sorts of symptom and that certain symptoms are common to different emotions; individuals vary greatly in the extent to which they present bodily symptoms both in comparison with other individuals and from time to time (Bridges, 1931, p. 198; Kenny, 1963, ch. 2). Hillman also describes the experimental attempts to induce emotion chemically. Some 'personal or individual' variable seems to intervene between drug and emotional reaction. In order to continue to think in terms of general hypotheses, psychologists have to take account of 'situation, meaning, [the] unconscious genetic constitution or . . . emotion itself as mood, suggestibility or personal idiosyncracy'. The fact is that once a substance gets into the body 'it is no longer . . . rightly a substance, but becomes an aspect of the body's life' (Hillman, 1960, pp. 123f.).

It is worth remarking, too, that affective phenomena are often said to vary generally in the extent to which they involve the body. Kolnai argues that disgust, for instance, is more intrinsically bodily than hatred and anger, even in the form of *moral* repugnance (1929, p. 121). Lersch points out that some affective phenomena *excite* us much more than others and tend to disturb the normally smooth running of the psyche. Such 'affects', as he calls them (anger is a member of this class), involve the 'experienced body' much more than other feelings (1954, p. 189). Later he points out that some moods do not involve the body much either; we are more inclined to think of them as atmospheric colourings of the soul (pp. 264f.).

Most English philosophers writing in recent years have strongly emphasised the difference between emotions and sensations. The latter are seen as purely bodily phenomena – that is, we experience aches, pains, pangs, and so on, *as* bodily phenomena – whereas the former are essentially intentional (directed towards an object). We shall see, however, that the intentional status even of phenomena like feelings of anger, irritation, and so on, is not nearly so obvious as some have thought, and there is in any case a large class of affective phenomena, including moods, which have no obvious intentionality about them at all. But the question clearly arises, can affective phenomena in general be clearly demarcated from 'mere' sensations (for clearly many affective phenomena *involve* them)?

Very few writers include sensations of hunger and thirst among affective phenomena. Hirst and Peters explicitly argue against this on the ground that they do not involve 'appraisals elicited by external conditions' (1970, p. 174). But nor do the sort of depression or the feeling of vital joy one may experience on getting out of bed after a night's sleep, and these are undoubtedly affective. They are, however, clearly states of the psyche. Though hunger and thirst are also states of *us* – it is right to stress this against certain types of dualist – they are more obviously states of a comparatively 'distant' part of us than moods, and are rather superficially felt in relation to our personal depths. Surely, one may feel inclined to argue, affective phenomena must be states or acts of the soul or psyche, and hence be rather more 'central' to us. But in affections the bodily phenomena are *expressive of the psyche*. There is no suggestion that this is true of hunger or thirst.

It is interesting, however, that Lersch includes hunger and thirst among affective *states* and both bodily and psychic *pain* within the category of movements of feeling. He analyses pain as follows (1954, pp. 194ff.). It has a meaning, for it is experienced as a disturbance in or threat to the basis of our existence. It is not merely a state, since *something* is experienced as the source of pain (even, presumably, 'something-I-know-not-what'). Nevertheless, the 'content' (we would say 'object') of pain is very hard to distinguish from its quality. It contains an impulse-component — one would like to be rid of it, but without knowing how. Most readers will probably feel that this applies to psychic pain rather better than to things like toothache. These, surely, have the same sort of 'distance' from the centre of the person that sensations of hunger and thirst do. Might not one also argue that hunger and thirst are not *merely* feeling-states but have a similar sort of meaning to pain, and that in hunger and thirst we 'know' at a primitive level that 'something' will satisfy them (does not a very young baby 'know' this?). Certainly, also, there is the impulse to satisfy one's needs. But why, then, exclude physical pain? Do we not all experience all these bodily phenomena (especially when the sensations are strong) as having the power — resistable only up to a point — to 'absorb' the psyche, so that they come to dominate our mental life until they are satisfied or removed?

Scheler solves these tangled problems with a theory of the stratification of feeling which includes feeling-states. His strata theory of the person is not quite the same as the one we are espousing in this work, but is more elaborate and based on his theory of value (though it shares certain features with the ideas of Lersch and Strasser). He sees four strata of affective phenomena: the sensible, the vital, the 'psychic' and the spiritual. Feelings of hunger, thirst, pleasure and pain belong to the sensible stratum. Such feelings are experienced as being related to our 'body-egos', are immediately subject to practical control, have essentially the shortest duration of any level of feeling, are extended and localised in the body, cannot be re-lived or anticipated, have no 'continuity of sense', are least disturbed by attention, and are essentially states with no intentionality (see Smith, 1977, pp. 105–7). Though one may take issue with some of these features, the picture is by and large a true one. What Scheler does not do is argue that bodily sensations are to be counted as affective phenomena. This is presupposed, so, from our point of view here, we are not taken much further.

It seems to me that the most important thing is to remember Lersch's remarks about psychological concepts. The world of inner experience simply cannot be understood as consisting of objects that 'give themselves to us' as of distinct kinds, like the worlds of living things or of artefacts. It is a matter of emphasis. Sensations of hunger and thirst, pleasure and pain, do now seem more like moods and feelings than they seem unlike them, now the reverse. I myself think that Scheler is probably right to classify them as a species or level of the Affective. But not much of importance hangs on whether he is right or not.

(6) Conclusion

Can 'the Affective', then, be satisfactorily demarcated? At the lower level of consciousness, that of 'feeling-awareness', it would appear not. Feeling, impulse and 'low-level' cognition form an indistinguishable whole, though more of a case can perhaps be made for separating cognition from feeling than for separating feeling from conation. Bodily involvement is a general feature of this level, though certain sorts of experience – sensations of pain, hunger, thirst, heat, cold, and so on – seem more bodily than others, and more 'remote' from the centre of the person. At the level of thought cognition and willing separate themselves firmly from one another. But feeling does not seem to belong to this level at all except in the comparatively 'bloodless' and 'cool' form of sentiments and attitudes (these are surely what Peters means by 'rational passions'), which lack the 'actuality' and 'warmth' of affectivity, but which are more closely related to and obviously dependent on it than cognition and willing.

Analysing the Affective Sphere Itself

(1) Differentiating Affective Phenomena

In a survey which included the study of pertinent works of over eighty philosophers and psychologists the following picture emerged: the notions of 'sentiment' and 'attitude' on the one hand (the two sometimes being taken as roughly equivalent, sometimes as distinct) and that of 'mood' on the other not only stood out clearly as fairly distinct phenomena within the affective field but were for the most part designated by the same terms as I have used myself (English translators presumably found it easy to render the ideas into English); the terms 'feeling' or 'feelings', 'emotion' or 'emotions', 'passion' or 'passions' (this last pair less frequent), and the much less frequent 'affect' or 'affects', however, were used of several fairly distinct phenomena, or could be seen as designating several salient points in the phenomenal field, and it is far less easy to see an emerging consensus as to which terms denote which phenomena.

Accordingly I have thought it best to proceed by listing the ten more or less distinct phenomena that it seemed to me the various writers consulted were talking about. These appeared to me, on further reflection, to reduce to four. It is clearly no accident that these are the four main phenomena analysed by Strasser in his *Phenomenology of Feeling* (1977). Whether this fact is due to my being too much influenced by Strasser or to the fact that the affective field proper (counting sentiments and attitudes as belonging to the level of thought) really *is* divided up in this way — or at least presents these four 'summits', like a mountain massif with four obvious peaks but more than four discernible protuberances — I leave it to the reader to judge.

The ten initial phenomena were (in random order):

(1) disturbance of judgement, 'functioning' or mood, together with attendant sensations,

(2) pleasure and pain, or feelings of 'hedonic tone',

(3) cognitively feeling things and situations (undiscriminatingly and vaguely),

(4) being bodily stirred up, together with some kind of apprehension of things,

(5) experience of impulse or conation, of being moved to action,

(6) affective tone, the experienced quality of one's inner state,

(7) being taken over, overwhelmed, regressing to a more primitive state,

(8) experience of being 'energised', facilitation of functioning, experiencing more intensively and concentratedly,

(9) being moved, stirred, excited, being responsive to things, sometimes as the result of 'appraising' them,

(10) Being attuned to, in the mood for, disposed towards things.

These ten phenomena seem, as I say, to distribute themselves either wholly or partly between four more basic and fundamental aspects of affective experience.

(A) Experiences of surrender of agency, of loss of control, of being overwhelmed, taken over, of being completely knocked off course (including both 1 and 7). Included here are paroxysms of infantile rage, being swept off one's feet by passionate love, being made prostrate by grief, maddened by pain, and so forth. Persons in the grip of strong, distorting passion often seem 'depersonalised', and we are apt to say they are 'not themselves'. We have seen that Peters had this group of

41

phenomena in mind in characterising emotion as 'passivity', and in fact quite a number of writers do reserve the term 'emotion' for these phenomena (see Strasser, 1977, pp. 264f.). Hillman quotes Jung as follows (1960, p. 61):

> As a matter of fact, an emotion is the intrusion of an unconscious personality. The unconscious contents it brings to light have a personal character, and it is merely because we never sum them up that we have not discovered this other character long ago. To the primitive mind a man who is seized by strong emotion is possessed by a devil or a spirit; and our language still expresses the same idea, at least metaphorically.

Findlay talks about 'warm', 'emotional' wants which, when thwarted, can ' "burst forth" into a range of manifestations, exceeding in force but having perhaps only a slender instrumental or other relevance to the objective pursued' (1961, p. 167).

It is worth following Strasser's analysis in detail here (1977, pp. 266–73). He gives an extended example of a young man being teased. At first the man reacts in a composed fashion: he chooses the appropriate movements of timidity or aggression on the basis of a 'pre-predicative global grasp of the situation' – that is, at the level of feeling-awareness. His behaviour is goal-oriented, and his (pre-predicative) grasp of it objective. His efforts are concentrated on conducting himself creditably. But gradually this proves too difficult and his 'vital attentiveness' slackens. The goal seems to recede from view, there seems no end to his ordeal in sight. Doubt sets in, he seems to have no way out; this brings on a further loss of power and self-confidence. Then a threshold is crossed. Composure yields to a 'formless, massive reaction' in which concrete possibilities are no longer perceived, the evil is experienced as overpowering, intentional contact with the environment is broken off, nothing is present to him except the all-encompassing evil. He bursts out blindly, launching himself wildly, arms flailing, in the general direction of his tormentors ('the evil'). All this betokens a surrender of spiritual or rational functioning, and of the secondary impulses of habit. 'Automatisms, reflexes and vegetable functions' take their place and there can be delusions, hallucinations and fainting fits (many of Sartre's examples of emotion are of this kind). But, Strasser insists, the 'abdica-tion' 'is still an expression of sovereign dignity', since it proclaims 'it is not in keeping with my dignity to be so bad a monarch'. Nevertheless, such an act could only be considered as a 'caricature of a sovereign deed'; hence emotion is 'an intermediate form between being overpowered and giving oneself as having-been-won-over'. But for man, such 'surrenders' betoken 'the end of behaviour', and hence no animal could ever experience an emotion. What we call 'emotional behaviour' is for them still purposeful. 'Being endangered by emotional

42

breakdown is just the price which man has to pay for his reason.' There are, in other words, situations that rational man cannot cope with. At such times he is unable to maintain the psychic distance that constitutes his rationality (see also Strasser, 1970). It is no accident that emotional outbursts are commoner among children who are only just beginning to live as rational or spiritual beings.

It is clear that not *all* instances of 'emotion', to adopt this name for this group of phenomena, need be accompanied by a surrender of quite this order. For instance, a person may fall deeply and passionately in love in circumstances that are completely inappropriate for one of his age, status, commitments, and so on. His passionate attachment brings about a complete 'restructuring' of his situation. Perhaps he gives up wife, possessions, job, respectability to go after his beloved. Certainly she has become the 'absolute good' for whose sake everything else must be revalued, but there will not be that complete surrender of rational and spiritual functioning that characterises certain seizures of rage or despair. He may, for instance, proceed perfectly 'rationally' to sell up, get a divorce, or send in his resignation, and so on. This is why Strasser argues that 'emotions always occur in the context of situations which . . . have an *existential* nature', where basic vital values are under threat (1970, p. 302). Passionate behaviour is treated by Strasser as a separate sub-phenomenon. I shall return to this highly significant affective phenomenon below (pp. 84-6).

(B) Being moved, stirred, excited, affected by an 'object' – perceived, remembered, or merely imagined – both mentally and physically (that is, 'totally'). Such 'feelings' represent the person's response to what has been apprehended. They include feelings of joy, wonder, delight, indignation, pity, admiration, disgust, and so on. They are normally intentional. In our discussion of Peters above we suggested that these feeling-responses always involve some sort of passivity. If one is to be 'affected' by what is essentially an 'object' for one – that is, 'outside' one – one has to hold oneself receptive, allow oneself to 'be moved' by the 'not-self'. All teachers of adolescents will recognise that kind of 'toughness' or 'indifference' many of them affect. Because they are finding their feet as independent individuals they will not allow themselves to be affected by the beautiful, interesting, or otherwise 'moving' objects their teachers indicate to them. It is easier to understand this if we grasp the element of 'voluntary passivity' intrinsic to 'being affected' (see also p. 99 below).

The degree to which one may be moved, stirred, or excited by things clearly varies enormously from person to person, occasion to occasion, object to object, and so on. If the affectivity is very great it may amount to a case of surrender of agency (A). Thus some of the phenomena comprised under *1* may have to be included here. Delight in something may become being obsessed by it, indignation at a person may become incoherent rage at him, and so on. It is perhaps because of this continuity that our culture has long been so suspicious of the 'passivity' involved in being affected by things, and has valued the 'stiff upper lip'. The involvement of the body has been experienced precisely as 'humiliating'; weeping in public, especially by men, has long been regarded as acutely embarrassing. But it seems quite clear that the passivity involved in wonder at the Niagara Falls, joy at the return of a loved one long absent, pity at the plight of victims of an accident, and so on, is a normal and healthy part of a properly human life, in a way that being overwhelmed, or abandoning control, is not. The former enhances humanity, the latter betokens a surrender of it. But the continuity between these two phenomena partly accounts for the differences of emphasis in Peters's and MacMurray's accounts of emotion.

It may be as well to insert at this point a brief discussion of 'sentiment' and 'attitude'. Examples of sentiments are love and hate; of attitudes, approval and disapproval. Sentiments are widely acknowledged as having a regulatory function in human life (Pradines, 1958, p. 191; Rawls, 1972, p. 479). Attitudes are seen as similar but more temporary (Rawls, ibid.; Strasser, 1977, p. 276). In particular their ordering function is directed to feelings and emotions. Ewing, for example, calls love and hate 'dispositions to have emotions' (1957, p. 67). Prescott (1938, p. 36) quotes Allport as saying:

An attitude is a mental and neural state of readiness, organized through experience, exerting a directive or dynamic influence upon the individual's response to all objects and situations with which it is related.

Midgley suggests that feelings and attitudes pass into one another: 'Fear, greed, and the like are *not* just feelings, sensations. They are attitudes' (1978, p. 345). To have a feeling, she goes on, is to have a pattern in one's life.

The relation between feeling-responses, attitudes and sentiments reflects the general relations between the level of feeling-awareness and the level of conceptual thought and will. The more attitudes and sentiments are envisaged instead of experiences of being moved, the more it is suggested that there is thought, deliberation, reflection, choice of purpose, and so on. Thus attitudes and sentiments can be completely 'cool', a matter of organisation and policy. Obviously a life whose 'affective' aspects showed no continuity or order would be chaotic and irrational, since the very possibility of significant experience shows that the world itself is ordered. Hence there must be a general desirability of transforming a life of isolated experiences of being affected into a life

44

organised by sentiments. The really fundamental question about how we are to see the relation between ordering sentiments and individual experiences concerns the *source* of the order: is this derived from 'reason', conceived of as quite distinct from the Affective, or is it derived from affectivity itself? Certainly sentiments and attitudes must *presuppose* feeling-experiences, if they are to be classed as affective, or quasi-affective, at all, but is the inspiration of their ordering to come from some non-affective, perhaps 'social', conception of reason, or from rational feeling itself?

Strasser appends to his discussion of attitudes and sentiments (here translated 'convictions') a brief account of 'comportment' and 'basic comportment'. Attitudes and sentiments presuppose thought, evaluation, and practical choice and thus influence the range and pattern of feeling-experience 'from above', as it were, because they involve the assent of the spiritual centre of the person, the 'I' who chooses and judges. But there is also a characteristic range and pattern of feeling arising from the 'given' (inherited or individual) predispositions of the person. Such a given 'cast of feeling' will in part account for the total style of a person's life, whether, for example, he organises it around the search for power, or for pleasure, or in a more contemplative or 'playful' style.

(C) Experiences of want, need, impulse, of seeking satisfaction or completion. In so far as one is talking merely of *affective* phenomena, this class excludes 'cool' wants, considered policies, and so on, just as the previous class excludes bare 'appraisals' (considered as *judgements*). But if the argument of this book is correct, 'cool' wants and so on are unintelligible except as developments of 'warm' wants. These experiences can also become more or less 'emotional'. That is, they can come to dominate and obsess one to the exclusion of everything else. In such cases we have attained the phenomenon of surrender of agency, or loss of control.

The phenomenon is described by Arnold and Gasson. They talk of 'the felt tendency toward an object judged suitable, or away from an object judged unsuitable, reinforced by specific bodily changes' (1954, pp. 203f.). In such experiences we are *aware* of an attraction, an impelling vital response, we recognise something as attractive or repulsive in relation to self. There is an intuitive judgement here.

It is important to stress the intuitive nature of such judgements. But in fact there are many occasions when the word 'judgement' seems out of place. One may well find oneself simply 'tending towards' something without even consciously knowing what it is. For instance, we come into a room while looking for, say, the cat, and find ourselves lingering, with a strong feeling of unease. This crystallises into the feeling that we really wanted to do something else. After a moment we find our attention solicited by a book lying on the window-sill, and recognise it as the book we needed half an hour ago and started to look for before being diverted on to other tasks.

It is significant that Arnold and Gasson identify *this* as emotion, seeming thus to ignore the central affective phenomenon (being affected). For such experiences are normally self-referential. It is *our* need, lack, want, and so on, that tends towards its object. By contrast, experiences of 'being affected' primarily stress our 'transcendence', that is, our capacity to be stirred by the 'not-self', to be 'taken out of ourselves' altogether. The willingness of philosophers and psychologists to accept experiences of being affected as a separate category may be closely bound up with their general understanding of values. Some seem to refer all values to the self, and thus by implication assimilate experiences of being affected to self-related experiences of impulse. Others tend to interpret them in terms of, and say they ought to be subordinated to, the idea of 'having reasons for action', where 'reasons' are understood in purely intellectual terms. But Peters himself certainly accepts the split between self-related and other-related 'emotions'.

This split is recognised by a great many thinkers. It forms the basis of, for example, Maslow's distinction between 'deficit needs', which we normally experience in terms of lack, and 'growth needs', normally experienced in terms of satisfaction (1968, ch. 3), or Scheler's distinction between vital values and spiritual values (1973, pp. 106–8), or MacMurray's distinction between response to self and response to the world, or Lersch's distinction between feeling-movements of 'living existence' and 'existence as an individual self' on the one hand and 'transcending' feeling-movements on the other (see below).

But it may well be asked why, if these thinkers can talk in terms of two types of feeling, or need, or value, I have spoken of a contrast between feeling-experience and experience of impulse. Are not these two phenomena things of a different order? It will, however, be remembered that conation is part of the experiential analysis of feeling. In being affected by something one is challenged, invited, or commanded to *do* something. Again, the reverse also obtains. The experience of impulse implies a feeling-response to something of value, even if it is not yet fully known. In thus claiming that experiences of being affected and experiences of impulse are two different sorts of thing, it would seem perhaps that I was merely stressing now one, now another, side of the same coin.

Nevertheless, the 'split' or discontinuity mentioned above occurs again and again in the literature in one form or another. And the analysis of what philosophers and psychologists do describe under the headings of 'feeling', 'emotion', 'affectivity', and so on, does reveal the existence of these two 'foci' around which the shifting and obscure phenomena seem to invite themselves to be organised. We may, perhaps, make sense of the correlation between self-directed feelings and experiences of impulse, and that between world-directed feelings and experiences of being affected, in this way. Because self-directed feelings, concerns, needs, values, and so on, are so much more urgent, pressing and 'foundational' in our experience (unless *they* are met, nothing higher can be), feeling passes directly into impulse, and the impulse gets effortlessly transformed into action. The 'invitations', 'challenges' and 'commandments' characteristic of higher value-experience are here in the normal case redundant, since the self offers no resistance. But it is easy for the person to 'get stuck' at the developmental level of 'deficit needs', 'vital values', self-concern, and so on. Not only does the self need to 'change gear', as it were, to tear itself away from itself; it also has to 'submit' to reality, to *let itself* be impinged on by the not-self, in order to be affected or moved by it. Hence, because of this slight resistance put up by our selves, we feel in some way *affected* by the value-objects of the world outside us *before* we are aware of the correlative impulse (in the normal case, that is). The slight reluctance that may attend our submission to the demands of reality *beyond* our immediate sphere of 'vital' or 'foundational' concern on the one hand; the effortless ease with which we respond 'practically' to the demands of our own bodily and psychic selves on the other; these two phenomena jointly seem to account for the experienced difference between 'being affected' and 'feeling an impulse'.

(D) Moods, the subjective colouring of experience. The most extensive treatment of moods I have come across, apart from those of Lersch and Strasser, is that of the German philosopher and educational writer O. F. Bollnow (1941). I shall therefore start by outlining his analysis. He calls moods 'life-feelings'. They are 'the lowest form of psychic life', and 'they present us with the simplest and most basic form in which human life becomes aware of itself – and moreover always with a particular "colouring", with a particular kind of valuation and attitude'. They can be thought of as variations of two fundamental moods – exaltation and depression. In contrast to feelings they are not intentional, but *states* of the psyche.

The German word for 'mood' is *Stimmung*, which means 'tuning'. Bollnow uses this etymological fact to highlight the element of 'attunement' that underlies 'being in the mood for'. In certain moods we are not 'attuned' to certain activities or persons. We cannot resonate in sympathy with them. But if we are not in the mood for some things, then we are attuned to others. Bollnow distinguishes three sorts of attunement – between inner and outer world, between bodily and psychic condition, between individual mental acts and the basic 'ground-tone' of the psyche.

At this foundational layer of experience the world is not yet 'objectified'. That is, we do not 'confront' it mentally as something distinct from ourselves. We are not yet 'distanced' from it. At this level we still live in the unbroken unity between self and world. The same colouring qualifies both us and the world. Hence, when we ascribe moods to the weather, to a landscape or a room, we are not essentially 'personifying' or speaking metaphorically; we may be quite literally describing our experience. This seems nonsensical to one who has adopted a 'theoretical', distanced, stance to things, whereas to one who is 'sunk' in his mood, who is living out of the deepest layer of conscious experience, it seems quite unextraordinary (Bollnow, 1941, pp. 17–22).

Because we are always in *some* mood or other, and therefore attuned to some things and not to others, moods determine in advance how life and the world appear to us. 'Only in an anxious mood will I encounter threatening things, and only if I am in a cheerful mood do cheering experiences seem to come to meet me' (ibid., p. 26). This explains why it is almost impossible to cheer up people who are really depressed, unless one can somehow awaken their interest. Although there are some things to which one can only be receptive in exalted and depressed moods respectively, the 'theoretical stance' towards things, in which one tries to be open to reality as such at the level of conceptual grasp and thought, is only open to one who is neither depressed nor exalted, but in a precarious kind of calm and peaceful mood. Bollnow also stresses that moral demands make no allowances for moods, implicitly requiring us to rise above ensnaring moods in which we might be tempted to wallow or remain lethargically sunk, and to encourage in ourselves 'good' moods rather than 'bad' – moods that make us receptive to other people and their needs rather than, say, to the atmospheric tone of inanimate nature or to our own psychic processes. Much of Bollnow's book is a critique of existentialism, which he charges with putting far too much stress on *Angst*, the mood of 'existential anxiety' which Kierkegaard and Heidegger emphasise. Although this mood is essential for a full grasp of man's finitude and weakness, and for inducing firmness and strength of character, it must be complemented by the more exalted and happy moods which alone enable man to unfold and develop himself.

How are moods related to other affective phenomena? Strong feelings, either powerful impulses or cases of being deeply moved, can themselves bring about a change of mood, as when we are shaken out of a perhaps 'shallow' depression by infectious gaiety or an attack on some vital interest which excites us to an immediate practical response. These facts lead Marshall to deny that moods are essentially objectless. He interprets them as 'extensions of affections beyond their original objects' (1968, pp. 244f.). If one denies that there ever *was* an affecting object that might have left one's present mood behind, he answers that there could have been an unnoticed object, or the object may not have been definite enough to be consciously apprehended. Alternatively one's state may not be a genuine mood (a state of soul, or mind, or psyche) but a psychophysically caused state. This last remark sounds odd coming from one who insists that the subject of affections is the *person*, and that affective reactions are both mental and physical (ibid., p. 247). It is clear that the reason for it is the concern to maintain the 'colonial' picture of reason (see above, p. 17). If object-directed psychic phenomena are somehow and in some cases dependent on, or influenced by, non-object-directed psychic phenomena, as well as the reverse case, then the lower levels of the psyche are being given an independent 'say' in things, which must influence our view of reason and all higher mental activity. This is the view we are trying to establish here, but which a great many philosophers still find unacceptable.

However, I end this section by citing Michael Tanner. Tanner claims, rightly in my view, that 'objectless' emotions have been seriously overlooked in recent (English) philosophy. 'The connexion between the emotional lives of almost everyone and the objects that those emotions have, when they have them, are loose to an extreme degree.' Most people lead totally disordered emotional lives, largely characterised by 'aimless or pointless feelings, existing prior to any object fitting or unfitting, and therefore always ready to latch onto the first even faintly plausible candidate for their expression' (1976–7, pp. 138ff.). Such unattached feelings we should see as the offshoots of moods. Thus there is constant 'two-way traffic' between mood on the one hand, and impulse or being affected on the other. And there is clearly an overlap between the phenomena.

Have we then succeeded in reducing the ten initial affective phenomena listed on page 41 to four? There is no difficulty about 7, and about fitting much of 1 into the same class of experiences of surrender of agency. Experiences of being affected clearly embrace 4 and 9. Some experiences of disturbance – 1 – seem not so much to amount to loss of control as to result from an 'interference' in experiences of being affected – or rather in the appropriate action that should follow these – by the *aspect* of being affected that attaches to experiences of impulse – 5 – which otherwise make up the third major category. That is, much disturbance results from the clash of self-related with other-related feelings. This leaves 2, 3, 6, 8, and 10. Mood-experience obviously embraces 6 and 10, and also 8, since such experiences are really a manifestation of elated and joyful, open moods. Pleasure and pain, or feelings of 'hedonic tone' – 2 – have always been difficult to classify. philosophically. But, in so far as these terms denote the qualitative aspect of experience they seem to belong either to the fourth (experience-colour) category, or with *4* and *9*. This leaves *3*, the cognitive feeling of things. By this is meant that our knowledge of things is based on a pre-conceptual feeling-awareness of them, in which 'cognition', 'feeling' and 'conation' are not yet distinct. But at this level there is no 'objectifying' either, which requires conceptual thought. Thus experience cannot be differentiated on the basis of its distinguishable objects. If it makes sense to talk of significant experience at all at this level (as opposed to a 'booming, buzzing confusion'), it must be differentiated because of its qualitative aspects, that is, its 'colouring'. We are clearly here within the sphere of mood or psychic 'colouring' and thus *3* also belongs within this wider class of affective phenomena.

(2)   The Idea of Feeling-Quality

This notion provides the acid test to distinguish between those philosophers whose interpretation of the Affective is in the end an 'intellectualist' one (with a 'colonialist' conception of reason), and those who grant the Affective an importance in its own right, seeing in it the necessary seed-bed of intellectual activity and the ultimate source of 'principles of reason'. The question which divides thinkers is this: can feelings be distinguished by their quality alone (as we can distinguish snooker balls by their colour), or is it impossible to distinguish them without referring to their objects and the circumstances of their arousal? In other words, is there a pre-conceptual knowledge of feeling? It is important to note that those who accept the idea of feeling-quality are not bound to claim that *all* differentiations of feeling that could be marked conceptually are actually discernible as differences of feeling-quality; only that some of them are and that all could be, given a vast and general increase in the relevant mental powers. They can accept that pre-conceptual awareness is often fleeting and uncertain in comparison with judgement, but they are convinced that some distinctions can be made out, a consideration which is reinforced by reflection on what must be the case if we are to make sense of certain other things.

We have already met some arguments against the existence of discernible feeling-quality. Bedford claimed, first, that the existence of it was not backed by his own experience, but made his case suspect by taking two closely related feelings, indignation and annoyance. But he seems wrong to me even here. Annoyance has about it a feeling of being personally thwarted; one's own plans or projects, and the feeling of one's own purposes as rolling forward unimpeded on their way, as smoothly developing according to plan, receive a set-back; there is a sense of a jolt, of being slightly obstructed or knocked off course. Indignation, however, contains a feeling of hostility flaring up and directing itself outwards; there is a feeling of gathering oneself to defend a principle; one is affronted not personally but on behalf of something to which respect or deference is due. And so on. Not everyone will agree with the detail of such descriptions. But, in so far as they join in at all and try to improve on them, they will surely be trying to recall typical *feelings* of annoyance and indignation and to capture their 'flavour' in words. Much poetry and serious novel writing is concerned with this sort of thing. It is, of course, true that one has to use words, refer to situations, and so on, to do it (though one must not forget that it can be done through mime, gesture, and so on, where the existence of rules linking experience and situation is far less obvious), but we all recognise the activity of trying to find words to convey the quality of felt experience.

The standard reply, of course, is not to deny that feelings exist, but to say that they are unknown and unknowable except in so far as they are described – and to do this one has to refer to their objects and the circumstances of their arousal. Against this one can at first return to the appeal to experience, and summon testimony from elsewhere. Hepburn, for example, in a discussion of 'emotional qualities' of works of art, insists that the feelings corresponding to these genuinely exist, and can be differentiated by us, even though they cannot be named (1965, pp. 196f.). He also appeals to the fact that we can rarely remember the precise feelings evoked by dreams, even though convinced of their individuality. Dreams are a good case because their conceptual content is often extremely inadequate. We know almost at once, when we start to describe the content of some dreams, that the attempt to put them in adequate words is hopeless. Marshall refers to 'affective colour', and points out that matching instances of this – which clearly presupposes discernibility – often replaces logical argument when one is in an affective state (1968, p. 246). Melden also suggests (1969, pp. 201ff.), as does Tanner (1976–7, p. 138), that 'free-floating' emotions may be fairly common. We may experience some anger, like some fear, without knowing what its object is, or being in the sort of situation that might well be expected to provoke it. Again, we make mistakes about the real object of our anger, suggesting that we do not always know we are angry because of the situation we are in (confronted by a hostile opponent, etc.) but seek a dynamically appropriate outlet or target (perhaps a totally innocent person) for a feeling we already 'know' on the basis of its quality, and only subsequently try to represent the object as *deserving* our anger.

But all these appeals to experience will be discounted and explained away by one convinced on independent grounds that there could not be such a thing as experience-quality. Such is the outcome of Bedford's second argument, which owes its origin to Wittgenstein. It goes like this: if 'anger' were the name of a feeling I could never teach a child how to use the word 'anger', since to do this I would have to be sure what his feelings were, which I cannot be, because I am not him. I could, in fact, only teach him how to use the word on the basis of 'outward' and 'public' evidence of anger. This argument does not in fact show that feeling-quality does not exist, only that it could not be used as a 'criterion' of any particular emotion. It is perfectly possible to argue that once one *has* learnt to use the word on the basis of outward evidence, one comes to connect it to the particular quality of one's private experience. But in any case one may dispute its premiss – that one cannot know what another person is feeling. The argument, as I claimed above, is a sceptical one, and is based on the presupposition that one cannot know anything that one cannot prove. It also presupposes an extreme individualism; that human beings are primarily isolated units, all social cohesion being 'additive', resulting from the consent of individuals to be bound by common rules for the sake of mutual advantage. Against this we must insist, largely following the insights of Scheler (1954, pt III, ch. 3), that man is primarily a social being, and that his individuality is subsequent to this, even though it is in the last analysis more important and also the goal of development. But at the basis of all contractual association of individuals is the sense of membership of one or more 'life communities'. But it is in life community, where there is a sense of communal togetherness ('we-experience'), common feeling, common purpose and a common mind, that a child first learns the language of emotion and feeling. At such levels of experience knowledge of other people's feelings is simply not a problem. A shared life, with its shared concerns and environment, is enough to ensure it. And the fact remains that we *do* normally divine without difficulty what our family, our friends and our close acquaintances (and very often people much less closely related to us than these) are feeling. The sceptical presuppositions must in the end be challenged by the presuppositions of ordinary interpersonal life.

It is interesting that J. N. Findlay, who is extremely eager to refute the idea of feeling-quality, does not himself employ the sceptical argument, but produces some ingenious, if not always absolutely perspicuous, arguments of his own. Findlay accepts that there is an internal 'feeling side' to emotion, but refuses to accept that we have here 'a mere case of quality' (1961, p. 171). His main strategy is to stress the cognitive aspects of feeling. Thus he discusses what differences there might be said to be between being cross and feeling cross, and interprets the distinction as follows: 'To *feel* cross is . . . not merely to *be* cross, but immediately to *know* or *perceive* that, and how, and with what, one is cross, and in what outward and inward ways one is showing this crossness' (p. 174). If one insists that something is nevertheless felt, his reply is that what one 'feels' just *is* the object of the crossness together with the multifarious ways in which one might behave crossly towards it 'held in dissolved unity' (p. 171). This not easily understandable idea is expressed again in his discussion of feelings of pleasure. He repeats the cognitive stress once more: '*Feelings* of pleasure . . . are our immediate awareness of the deep *fit* between wants and circumstances', and goes on: 'the glow or sweetness or bloom which seems the heart of the matter in our state of felt pleasure' – we might claim that this is a reference to feeling-quality – 'can be none other than the condensing power of conscious experience, its ability to hold complex relationships in dissolved suspension, which we again and again encounter in the life of the mind' (ibid., p. 177).

Findlay thus interprets what common sense normally regards as the 'flavour' or 'atmosphere' of affective experience as a condensation of the objects and possible associated impulses of such experience. Why, then, might not one equally argue that the objects and possible associated impulses were 'expansions' rather than condensations; that the objects of emotions were the actual or explicit developments or realisations of what was already somehow implicitly pre-cognised in the feelings, and the possible associated impulses the 'natural' or appropriate practical unfoldings of what was already pre-given in germ? It is surely undeniable that what can be seen as a condensed form of some given original thing can itself be the original thing of which this other thing is an expansion. One will choose the alternative that coheres best with the remaining data.

Findlay also argues that if pleasure and displeasure were 'peculiar *qualities* of experience . . . it would be a gross, empirical accident that we uniformly sought the one and avoided the other' (loc. cit.). In fact 'the notion of pleasure . . . has the notion of a want practically built into it . . . and this could *not* be the case were it some simple empirical quality' (ibid., p. 178). But one may accept the intimate connection between pleasure and wanting without accepting the conclusion. For pleasure is a generic term, which covers all those specific qualities which we do in fact want to come into contact with. The fact that we *necessarily* want pleasure does not mean that we necessarily want the specific qualities of feeling produced by caviare, sherry, French perfume, or silk underclothes. Nor is one necessarily committed to hedonism or the moral theory that 'pleasure' is the only thing that really motivates us by accepting this, as Findlay implies. And one may again wonder, as I did in the case of Peters above, what the ideas of 'strong' and 'weak' feeling (which he mentions several times) mean if there is no feeling-quality for them to refer to.

It is interesting to note the results of experiments reported by W. B. Cannon (1927, p. 49). In this work attempts were made to produce emotions artificially by inducing the visceral changes characteristic of strong emotions. The attempts failed, but did produce the *sensations* typical of emotion, together with reports from the subjects that it was *as if* they were feeling certain emotions. Such sensations could not possibly be interpreted in Findlay's way. We may also note that Melden accepts the existence of feeling-qualities, though does not think that there are strong enough correlations between particular feelings and particular emotions to make the former a reliable guide to the latter. But his reason does not seem very compelling. 'Anger', he writes, 'can be many things in the life of the same person' – for instance, depressing, exhilarating, annoying, distasteful, to be relished or enjoyed (1969, p. 204). But *whether* anger depresses, exhilarates, annoys, and so on, depends on whether one is able to express it or not, whether one approves or disapproves of one's outburst, whether it results in harm or grief to a loved person, and so on. Anger, that is, is always based on the same sort of feeling (assuming that it is the the same *kind* of anger), but one's own anger may be mingled with other feelings, or give rise to new feelings, and so on.

An important argument in favour of the existence of discernible feeling-quality concerns the way values are given to us. Rawls, representing a pronouncedly 'intellectualistic' approach to the mind, holds that moral feelings (guilt, shame, remorse) are distinguished from non-moral by the type of *explanation* required for having one (1972, pp. 480ff.). Indeed, according to him, a man may not *be* guilty of an act, and yet be correctly said to *feel* guilty, 'since his explanation is of the right sort'. However, if we ask for the *origin* of the different sorts of explanations or reasons that, according to Rawls and those who think like him, are the criteria of different sorts of feelings, we seem in the end – unless we think that 'conceptual schemes' and so forth simply dropped from heaven – to be forced back to feeling itself. Edith Stein accepts that values are 'constituted' in feeling, and points out that differences in types of value (hedonic, vital, aesthetic, moral) are in the end based on differences in the 'material' of value-cognition, in other words on feeling-quality (1970, p. 146). As Roman Ingarden points out in a general discussion of values, we *do* distinguish between values and between kinds of values, and agree with one another in so doing, and yet have no completely acceptable public criteria to rely on. Our discrimination is based on our feeling-apprehension of differences in their *qualitative* nature. We certainly 'feel' the difference between, say, aesthetic and moral beauty, and between moral and 'vital' nobility, and, although we can no doubt say quite a lot about these values and disvalues, the surest way we have to fasten on and communicate their differences is to try to recall situations when we have been confronted by them directly and then convey, by metaphor and analogy, the qualitative nature of the relevant feeling-experiences.

Nevertheless, as I have already conceded, it would clearly be absurd to claim that we could normally do without the 'situation' and 'object' aspects of feeling in identifying them. This is partly due to the fact that language itself requires more or less public criteria if it is to be an efficient means of communication. It is also due to man's need to operate at the level of conceptual thought as well as that of feeling-awareness. But there are two main reasons for insisting on feeling-quality. The needs to communicate and to think about (or 'examine') one's own feelings in general terms are important. But so are the needs to 'live out of' our depths and to confront our feelings as they really are. To insist that a large number of feelings, perhaps the vast majority, cannot be adequately conceptualised helps us to see how *both* these requirements are possible. Secondly, it is important to emphasise that every single act, and every single human experience, *originates* in and develops from feeling, and that human life must keep in touch with the life of feeling if it is not to suffer grave distortion and damage.

A note on 'primary emotion' and its development. It may be as well to add at this point a few remarks about the notion of 'primary' emotion. A large number of writers on emotion have produced confident or tentative lists of basic or fundamental emotions or feelings. Shand suggests fear, anger, disgust, curiosity, joy, 'sorrow-repugnance-aversion', self-display and self-abasement (1914, pp. 57ff.). Descartes lists six primitive passions: wonder, love, hatred, desire, joy, sadness (1649, section LXIX). All the others are made up, or are 'species', of these. Hillman quotes H. F. Harlow and R. Stagner who claim that emotions are 'conditioned' on the basis of four fundamental feeling-tones: pleasure, unpleasure, excitement, depression (Hillman, 1960, p. 147). Bridges thinks there is one basic emotion present at birth: excitement, which progressively develops into distress, excitement and delight, then into fear, anger, distress, excitement, delight, joy, affection, and so on, new emotions being progressively differentiated out (1931, p. 209). Other candidates for a single aboriginal emotion are spasm, startle, *étonnement* and *choc* (Hillman, 1960, p. 155). Strasser suggests three (or six) basic emotional tendencies: 'the inborn desire for pleasure and that of turning against the one who puts an obstacle in the way of satisfying that craving', 'the innate need for security, and aversion for what causes dread' and 'the desire for power and the tendency to overcome powerlessness' (1969, pp. 87f.). Kenny reports J. B. Watson as holding that there are three basic emotional behaviour-patterns: fear, rage and love (1963, p. 42). Lastly, Shibles mentions C. Izard's nine 'fundamental emotions': interest, joy, surprise, distress, anger, disgust, contempt, shame, fear (Shibles, 1974, p. 189).

What exactly does all this signify? First, there are the simple observations (or hypotheses) that certain emotions or feelings appear before all others in the individual's life. Secondly, there is the attempt to classify feelings, to lay bare the structure of feeling. The suggestion, here, is that a person who cannot feel one of the basic emotions is not fully developed as a human being. But how can emotions also be said to 'develop' out of each other? If we look once more at Bridges's developing list we can see that the development is a refinement or sharpening, which, the world being what it is, has a kind of inevitability about it. Clearly there is more than one kind of excitement; clearly again there is more than one kind of distress and delight; and so on. But why is such a development somehow inevitable? The rough answer is this: man is essentially a being who is open to the world. The development of his emotional life will therefore be dictated by the nature of the world itself, and the range of his feelings will correspond to the degree to which he is able to respond to it, first, inevitably, in terms of his own vital needs, but then, increasingly, in terms of its own nature, to which he is essentially attuned. But, from the subjective point of view, his ability to experience ever more refined and sharpened or concentrated feelings can be compared to his ability to discriminate more and more between colours. First come the primary colours, then the four or five other 'major' colours and then progressively more and more shades and hues. It is as though the original stock of feeling-quality were essentially dynamic in nature; as the individual comes to differentiate between the various shades of his feeling he finds more and more directions for his life. Clearly the only limits to this developing discrimination are the individual's own powers and the use he makes of them.

4

The Place of Feeling in the Human Economy and its Significance for Human Life

The Question of Stratification

It should now be clear, I hope, that one cannot really understand the human mind without accepting its stratified nature. Certainly it is impossible to make this absolutely clear; nor can one 'prove' it by means of tight logical argument or the analysis of ordinary language. The picture is bound to be conveyed through metaphor, and the perhaps question-begging descriptions of the everyday phenomena of experience. It must also be stressed that the picture of mental strata cannot have that geological neatness or definiteness it inevitably conjures up. The 'layers' are much more like the bands of colour in a rainbow, which we are accustomed to distinguish but which in fact form a continuum. Thus, though we may *talk* of the presence or absence of conceptual thinking, it is impossible to say or even to imagine at what point feeling-awareness gives place to experience mediated through concepts.

Casual talk of higher and lower levels, of one thing developing out of another, and so on, is very common in philosophical psychology. Pradines talks of passions lifting sentiments or feelings 'to the level of reason', of emotions tending 'to lower sentiments to the level of reflex' (1958, p. 197). Aschenbrenner says appetitions belong to 'the basic animal stratum of our own being', and that emotive responses are 'built upon them'; appraisals, which introduce reasons, are a higher step still (1971, pp. 40–8). The eighteenth-century philosopher Thomas Reid produces four distinct principles of action which are clearly to be understood in terms of ascent to something higher. They are 'instinct or habit', 'appetite', 'desire' and 'affection' (1788, essay III).

57

However, not many thinkers explicitly devote themselves to the question. R. S. Peters, as we have seen, has done so, but his analysis invites us to take the lower levels as stages to be passed through and, ideally, left behind for ever, rather than as an account of the necessary foundations of all minds and all acts. Nevertheless, the details of his first and third stages are very similar to those of Lersch's and Strasser's two main conscious stages.

Lersch lists three sorts of considerations to support intuitions about strata (1954, pp. 74f.). First, there are the ideas of Freudian psychology, with its three strata of id, ego and superego, the ego only accepting into consciousness from the id what the norms of the superego allow. There is also the idea of the 'pre-conscious', which we seem to be able almost to observe as when mild pain drifts into and out of consciousness or, when we are tired, we sometimes 'lose sight' of the content of the book we nevertheless continue to read. Langer also uses this fact to defend the idea of the subconscious (1967, Vol. I, p. 22):

It is this transiency and general lability of the psychical phase [that is, the actual 'being-felt-ness' of vital processes and activities] that accounts for the importance of pre-conscious processes in the construction of such elaborate phenomena as ideas, intentions, images and fantasies, and makes it not only reasonable but obvious that they are rooted in the fabric of totally unfelt activities which Freud reified with the substantive term 'the Unconscious'.

Lersch's second appeal is to brain research, which seems to show that perception, language, intelligence, memory and purposive action are associated with the cerebrum, and affectivity, drives and feelings with developmentally older parts of the brain. In other words, there are physiological strata that seem to be roughly correlated with the experienced strata of consciousness (though for a more cautious appraisal of the evidence see, for example, Strongman, 1973, p. 58).

Lastly, Lersch appeals to Nicolai Hartmann's ontology and metaphysics, in which a stratified theory of reality in general is defended. Polanyi provides a more accessible version of such an approach for English readers (1958). The fundamental idea is that the higher depends materially on the lower (e.g. mind depends on body) but cannot be reduced to it, since a new metaphysically significant ordering principle has to be invoked to understand it (see also below, pp. 60f).

Lersch also points to the very widespread occurrence, both in our own and in other cultures, of a sort of pre-scientific version of strata theory, according to which the lower part of the trunk (the 'belly') is taken to be the seat of elementary life-drives (hunger, thirst, sexual desire), the breast, including the lungs and heart, is taken to be the seat of emotions and feeling, and the head of thinking and willing (1954, p. 81). Plato provides a more sophisticated version of these ideas.

According to Lersch there are three strata of the psyche: the 'life-ground', entirely unconscious but perhaps indirectly accessible through dreams and analysis, the 'endothymic ground' and the 'personal superstructure'. Very roughly, the endothymic ground is the level of conscious experience (though it shades off into unconsciousness – the 'pre-conscious'), the personal superstructure the level of what the person does with or in response to experience. Thus, judged with reference to each other – for the notions of passivity and activity are relative where persons are concerned (Dunlop, 1977, p. 242) – the endothymic ground is a place of passivity, the personal superstructure one of activity. In the former we are subject to changes of mood, we are moved or affected by things we encounter, we are driven, pulled and summoned by impulses and pressures from within, invitations and demands from without; in the latter we order and question our cognitions, challenge experienced validities, 'look again' at invitations and demands, pressures and impulses, either more or less responsibly choosing between them or letting things simply 'take their course'.

Scheler provides perhaps the best purely phenomenological indication of the necessity for accepting some sort of stratification of the self. Strasser summarises the argument clearly as follows (1977, p. 57):

> How else would one explain the fact that . . . a man drinks a glass of wine in an unhappy mood and . . . is capable of consciously enjoying the bouquet of the wine? . . . Both are given in experience at the same time: the basic unhappy disposition and the appreciative delight in the fine taste. Both experiences melt completely into each other, but are embedded as distinct presences in the total experience. If the sensory enjoyment and the 'deep' maldisposition lay on the same level, then they must cancel out one another.

The reader will easily be able to think of further examples, coming, perhaps, under the headings of guilty pleasures, the sadness of victory, the agony of athletic achievement, the martyr's bliss, and so on, where consciousness may be filled with both positive and negative feelings and where it is natural to account for our state in terms of levels and depth. Strasser thus describes the idea of stratification as a 'material a priori presupposition for a complete phenomenological doctrine of man' (ibid.).

Scheler's ideas on the stratification of feeling are well summarised and discussed by Quentin Smith (1977) and Strasser (1977, pp. 52–63). Scheler also puts forward stratification theories of value (1973, pp. 105–8) and of levels of psychic activity in animals and men (1961). Indeed, the idea of stratification occurs throughout his voluminous works. But because his ideas are always developing he is not the easiest writer to summarise if one tries to capture his thought as a whole. I shall therefore turn straight to Strasser, whose debt to Scheler – and also to Lersch – is great, but who provides a very much more satisfactory theoretical account of stratification than either.

Strasser's own account of 'strata theory' (1977, pp. 149–73) starts with a reminder of the astonishing contrast which extreme emotional excitement, or the 'surrender of agency', offers to the calm, rational and ordering aspect of human being. How can 'pathos' and 'logos' both be present in a person, who is at the same time a unity? To interpret 'logos' and 'pathos' as two rival principles on one level would be to deny the unity. To make logos subordinate to pathos would be to reduce rational thought to a mere 'epiphenomenon', a sort of idle embellishment to the 'real' work of feeling. Pathos, then must be subordinate. But how? As logos's 'instrument'? But feeling (pathos) has a centrality in human experience that speaks against this. Again, it is an active principle (in relation to human being as a whole) with a vital part of its own to play in the human economy. Thirdly, if it is an instrument, how could it be thought to *conflict* with logos? The clue to the relation is Aristotle's idea of 'political or royal rule . . . the relation of the citizen to his lawful government'. It is, in a word, 'hierarchic'. In such a relation the levels are ontologically distinct (they have their own distinct nature), the higher levels are 'eidetically' autonomous (they have their own 'eidos' or form), the lower levels providing the necessary but not sufficient condition for their existence, and the subordination of the lower levels 'is an activity of the living individual and not that of one particular level'. Any impairment of functioning of lower levels (in this case the bodily level, or again the level of pathos) inhibits the development of higher levels and may lead to breakdown.

This idea of development is crucial for understanding the 'vertical binding' of the strata. To say that the higher arises from the lower is to talk of 'an activity of the living individual' (which may fail) and not to indicate a merely causal relation. The higher level is, first, not *totally* explained in terms of the lower, and is, secondly, *intelligibly* connected to it, since 'bios' (Lersch's 'life-ground'), pathos and logos must ultimately be understood as levels of a *whole*. In fact there must be laws of development governing the coming into being of *all* levels. Such laws must find room for a principle that shapes the whole course of development from the beginning. 'While the bridge from Bios to Pathos is built, the direction towards the still-not-factually-present Logos is already being followed'; in Polanyi's terms, the bias towards *meaning* is present in nature from the very start (see the section 'Is evolution an achievement?' in Polanyi, 1973, pp. 382–90).

These ideas enable us to conceive of the *wholeness* of human being as prior to the principles governing the levels of that being. Animals and humans develop into the two or three levels that respectively constitute them through the principle of 'animation'. This 'metaphysical notion' is 'a principle of being which must be introduced for the sake of the intelligibility of a region of being'. Without it strata theory, itself justified phenomenologically, would be unintelligible. We should add here that, for Strasser, strata theory does not just apply to the whole being of man but to every human act. 'At every moment . . . I am engaged in development – from Bios through Pathos to Logos.' All man's thoughts and decisions have their origin in unconscious life; all the blind urges and tendencies of this stratum strive upwards towards the clarity and precision of rational thought and will. At the same time activity at the level of logos – or its effects – somehow filters back down again to the lower levels. The unity and wholeness of the person must be taken seriously.

The Place of the Affective in the 'Human Economy'

This question is frequently discussed from within some established science, such as neurophysiology, or evolutionary biology, or psychoanalysis, whose range of interest is restricted. But philosophy is the critical examination of the whole of human experience. Worthwhile philosophical answers to our question must both account for the way emotion and feeling present themselves to us and also acknowledge their subjective significance in life. William James's well-known theory about the 'coarser' emotions – that they are nothing other than our feelings of the bodily changes that directly follow certain perceptions (1950, Vol. II, p. 449) – certainly admits them as subjective phenomena but makes them sound rather trivial and unimportant. The theory is, in any case, inadequate on other grounds (see, for example, Lehmann, 1914, and Cannon, 1927).

Many accounts by philosophers trained in the conceptual analytic tradition also disappoint those who see philosophy as a human rather than a technical discipline. Even Peters, with his healthy insistence on passivity and on 'levels of life', fails in the end to give emotion any more positive role in human life than that of stoking the fires of rational thought. Warren Shibles, an American linguistic philosopher, denies it even this auxiliary role. According to him 'emotion is a verbal skill. It involves not introspection . . . but rather looking at our language' (1974, p. 29). 'Emotion, in itself, is a fiction. Emotions are nothing in themselves. They reduce to non-emotion terms' (ibid., p. 8). 'Emotion is assessment which guides feeling' (p. 17). The trouble is, he regards feeling as 'largely sensation or bodily state' (p. 141). The idea that feeling is itself an essential form of cognition, and that all goodness, beauty and even truth are somehow first given to us in feeling, is quite foreign to him. His refusal to take the dynamic and developmental aspects of emotion and feeling seriously (any talk of 'energy' is castigated as commission of the 'naming fallacy'), or to examine the nature of feeling as it deserves, gives an air of triviality and pedantry to his account. The fact is that the philosophical method espoused by Shibles and others simply is not capable of being used to illuminate our fundamental intuitions in this field. Sometimes it pretends there is really nothing to say; at others it presses its nose impotently against the glass case of its own assumptions and, by means of incidental hints and asides, expresses its longing to handle the really important things it cannot reach.

One of the most interesting and profound attempts to give a full and proper answer to the question of emotion's place in human life is that of Sartre. He makes it quite clear that his 'outline of a theory' not only contains an answer to the question 'what is emotion?', but also to the question about its significance for man, and of what it has to tell us about human nature (1948, p. 15). In the first place, he says, emotion is unreflective. It is primarily 'consciousness of the world' without any additional consciousness of one's own mental state or mental directedness (ibid., p. 50). 'Emotion is a certain way of apprehending the world' (compare Peters and MacMurray), but when I am, say, afraid I am not aware of my fear but of what I am afraid of. Emotion is also 'a transformation of the world'. It occurs when things get too difficult to cope with in the normal way. But sometimes, in such situations, 'we must act, so we try to change the world, that is, to live as if the connection between things and their potentialities were not ruled by deterministic processes, but by magic' (p. 58). This change, which, we must not forget, Sartre thinks that we bring about without knowing that we are doing so, is accomplished by means of the body. Thus emotions are 'tantamount to setting up a magical world by using the body as a means of incantation' (p. 70). Naturally he gives examples. We may faint with fear, thus magically 'annihilating' ourselves 'in order to annihilate the object' as well. We are numb with grief, and withdraw deep into ourselves, 'in such a way that the universe no longer requires anything of us' (pp. 64f.). We go wild with joy at the approach of a long-awaited relative or friend; our extravagant bodily behaviour 'tends by incantation to realize the possession of the desired object as instantaneous totality', seeking to anticipate a security of possession that is illusory. Then again in 'false' joy and 'false' sadness, in which our bodies mime the originals, 'we intend magically to invest real objects with certain qualities [which are] false'. 'True' emotion, however, is accompanied by belief. 'The qualities conferred upon objects are taken as true qualities'. The seriousness of all this is shown by our bodily involvement: *'in order to believe* in magical behaviour it is necessary to be highly disturbed'. Thus we really 'live' the magical world we have set up. Emotion thus represents the 'degradation' of consciousness (pp. 72ff.). Rather than admit that 'consciousness is caught in its own trap', we try to live as though it were objects that 'captivated' *us*. We can only get free through 'purifying reflection or a total disappearance of the affecting situation'. The act of 'purifying reflection' would show us that we had all along been unreflectively and mistakenly *constructing* this world of emotion in which we were ensnared. Sartre emphasises that 'emotional qualities' (we would call them values and disvalues), such as 'the horrible', are only 'syntheses' of here-and-now particular experiences projected on the world as permanent objective qualities. Reflection would destroy emotion's pretensions to be 'intuition[s] of the absolute' (pp. 79ff.).

However, there is a range of affective phenomena that cannot be conceived of in this way. 'For example, suddenly a grinning face appears flattened against the window pane; I feel invaded by terror.' Such a 'perception of the *horrible* . . . is not accompanied by flight or fainting [or] even by impulsions to flight . . . There is no behaviour to take hold of.' In such cases it is not that consciousness 'abruptly transforms the determined world in which we live into a magical world', but that 'this world . . . sometimes reveals itself to consciousness as magical . . . Indeed, we need not believe that the magical is an ephemeral quality which we impose upon the world as our moods dictate. Here is an existential structure of the world which is magical.' Sartre proceeds to point out that the world of interpersonal relations is essentially magical. Man's attempts to see it deterministically are doomed to failure. Sooner or later consciousness inevitably 'seize[s] upon the magical as magical [and] forcibly live[s] it as such'. Thus there are two forms of emotion. In one 'it is we who constitute the magic of the world to replace a deterministic activity which cannot be realized'. In the other 'it is the world itself which abruptly reveals itself as being magical'. There are also intermediate cases − mixtures of the two (pp. 82ff.).

Sartre's answer to the question of the place of the Affective − or rather, of 'emotion' − in the human economy is thus as follows: it is the means by which consciousness returns 'to the magical attitude, one of the great attitudes which are essential to it, with appearance of the correlative world, the magical world' (pp. 90f.).

Sartre is clearly not writing about the Affective as a whole. There is no consideration of non-intentional phenomena here, or of affective phenomena that pre-eminently concern desire or impulse (experienced as pressure from within) as opposed to those that give themselves to us primarily in terms of response to things outside us. Nevertheless, the 'sketch' seems to claim, by implication, a wider significance, and to interpret affectivity as such. Much of what he says illuminates the phenomenon of 'surrender of agency', but the adequacy of the interpretation as a whole partly depends on the meaning of the word 'essential' in the last quotation. If 'the magical attitude' – which amounts, in our own terms, to experiencing the world as itself invested with value and disvalue – is 'essential', then it would seem that Sartre considered it legitimate. Yet, first, it is supposed to involve a 'degradation of consciousness'. Secondly, Sartre says that although the magical attitude will sometimes stand up to reflection, and we shall conclude 'I am angry *because* it is hateful', such reflection is 'accessory'; pure reflection will conclude 'I find it hateful *because* I am angry' (p. 91) – which amounts, as it seems, to a rejection of the magical attitude and an approval of such rejection. Thirdly, the very term 'magical' suggests illegitimacy. It is hard not to conclude, especially in the light of Sartre's whole *œuvre*, that the 'essential' is an ironic concession to human frailty and that the ideal is complete resistance to the attitude. In any case one may well feel that Sartre simply has not made out his case for the 'two forms of emotion'. For if I construct the world of magic on some occasions, why not on all? Do I not *choose* to see the world as magical in the case of the grinning face at the window? This is surely as much a 'choice' as some of the choices described as such in Sartre's later works. As Fell suggests (1965, pp. 205f.), it prompts the question: why *suffer* this intrusion? Why not work a little magic to dissolve it (a fainting fit, perhaps)? But there is no space here for detailed criticism, or indeed for acknowledging in any other than very general terms the richness and fascination of Sartre's account. If one could take his 'essential' seriously, understanding by it something to be encouraged and striven for because of its promise of human wholeness and completion, and interpret the world of magic as the world of values, which can indeed, as Sartre correctly saw, only be fully accessible to us if we approach it non-instrumentally, then his answer to our question would be similar to MacMurray's, and, like his, incomplete rather than inadequate. But, as it is, it is too closely intertwined with his distortingly one-sided understanding of human nature. (Many of the essential critical points are made by Fell and Strasser: see Fell, 1965; Strasser, 1977, ch. 2).

Another interesting attempt to answer our question – though, again, confined to 'emotion', and not applying to the whole range of affective phenomena – is that of James Hillman. After an impressively thorough survey and classification of theories of emotion Hillman not surprisingly concludes that an adequate theory must see it from various points of view. So he adopts an Aristotelian 'four causes' model to aid our understanding (1960, pp. 247–9). In answer to the question: what initiates emotion, or brings it about? (efficient cause), he says 'there is emotion because the world is being apprehended and lived through a symbol' (i.e. we experience the world as *significant;* ibid., p. 248). If one asks:

'what is the nature, the stuff of emotion?' (material cause), the answer is: energy, known in its bodily manifestations and mental representations (p. 266). The formal cause, which defines emotion, or makes it what it is, is the soul or psyche itself: 'emotion is a total pattern of the soul', which naturally includes feeling as well as other elements (p. 269). The final cause, which is the answer to the question about the purpose or end of emotion, is 'transformation' (p. 278). Emotion changes us. How? Whether or not its *expression* is judged good in some respect or other (it may, for example, be socially frowned on, or disturb other people), it is always good in itself; the transformation is bound to improve us (p. 283):

> My will is frustrated; there is conflict, disorder and unconsciousness. I have fallen into my ancestral past and into my flesh. Yet in this fall I am reunited with the world, with my body, with the objective psyche and with a will and reason beyond my own doing. I am improved because I live what I am.

Certainly there can be emotional outbursts and excesses (in our terms, there can be surrender of agency), but these are the result of a sudden 'abdication' after attempts to suppress emotion, and are neither expressions of the whole psyche nor responses to symbols or images. They result from a failure of consciousness 'to accept emotion and to live it' (p. 285). Psychic disorder in general, however, is not necessarily bad, since it may be necessary if a new stage of growth is to be initiated. Only an erroneous 'homoestatic', that is, non-developmental model of the person could ignore this (pp. 209–11). For though emotional upset may result from 'partial' living, it can lead to a renewal of wholeness, as the personal centre regains contact with the heart of itself. Emotion proper, however, is 'that transformation of the energy of the conventional set which is achieved by the whole psyche and which is initiated by a symbol' (p. 287).

Hillman ends his account with a reference to Plato's *Phaedrus*, in which the soul is likened to 'a winged charioteer and his team acting together'. One of the two horses of the team, says Plato, is 'good and of noble stock' (reason) and the other is 'the opposite in every way'. This has been traditionally identified with emotion. The implication of the likeness is that the soul will only attain the heavenly regions it aspires to if it becomes the absolute master of the 'dark horse', which is always trying to drag it downwards, by application of the whip (Plato, *Phaedrus*, sections 246ff.). Hillman suggests that, instead, the central part of the self should learn to use the reins properly, and give the dark horse its head. 'We are reined to the horse, it to us. This is emotional existence, driving and being driven, the true image of *homo patiens*' (p. 289). Thus for Hillman the emotional life is the most authentic life, because in submitting to it (*homo patiens*) one is united with one's real self, which is, in turn, part of a larger whole and a larger life (see the 'will and reason beyond my own doing' above – a reference to Jung's theory of the collective unconscious, the source of much human wisdom). But emotional excess is not directly fruitful, or necessarily 'adaptive' in this way. The place of true emotion in the human economy seems to be to change a person for the better by strengthening the bond with the true self and weakening the seductive influence of the intellect or any other 'part-function' of the psychic life. The stress is very much on wholeness.

Hillman's account, though extremely suggestive and important, is in the end partial. It does not apply to non-intentional phenomena, nor is it clear how it could be fitted into a total picture of consciousness, which also finds a place for thought, 'reason' and desire. It seems also excessively optimistic. 'Emotion is always good' is only plausible if one discounts the evidence of human splitness, of a divisiveness at the centre of the psyche. It seems also to have little place for human transcendence, for man's need to find the meaning of his life outside himself – though it is certainly true that the Jungian element in Hillman's thought, which sees some of this 'transcendence' in our access to the 'collective unconscious', is a kind of substitute for this. The 'inner' and the 'outer' are, admittedly, at their extremes, paradoxically similar. However, there is no sense in his work that affective phenomena are cognitive vehicles of the values of the world outside us. His account, taken as a whole, is too 'vitalistic', and has no obvious place for spiritual phenomena in human life.

Lersch's account of the 'endothymic ground' and its significance is part of a much wider endeavour – to exhibit the structure of the human person as a whole. Thus the links between aspects of affectivity and the relations between it and other aspects or functions of the psyche are for the most part made explicit.

Experiences of impulse, most generally characterised by a feeling of need or lack, are, according to Lersch, the experienced inner side of the 'law of communication', the essential interrelationship between living thing and its environment in the matter of self-preservation, self-unfolding and self-fashioning. Every experience of need is thus also a dim and obscure anticipation of the future, of a 'something' that will satisfy it (Lersch, 1954, p. 95). But impulses and feelings are very closely bound up with each other. What we 'take in' from the outer world is strongly conditioned by impulse, which then finds its 'echo' in experiences of being affected. Thus what moves us are those aspects of the world that we impulsively looked for (ibid., pp. 180f.). 'In experiences of being moved we experience the relation in which the contents of the objectively disclosed world stand to the various themes of our conations' (p. 183).

We shall return to Lersch's analysis of the 'structure of feeling' in a later section. Let it suffice to say here that both impulses and feeling-movements reveal the three themes of pre-individual existence, existence as an individual and transcending existence (in which one reaches out beyond oneself in response to the world outside one). The existence of conations and feeling-movements that concern the 'not-self' reveal that man is not only a living and a self-concerned being, but also 'essentially a spiritual being'. What is more (p. 245):

> The movements of conscience [for example, remorse] show that man's existence is not given to him as a fact of life, as it is to a plant, and that he does not merely have to provide for it by staying alive, like an animal, but that it is really entrusted to him, and that he is appointed to play his part in the realisation of meaning in the world.

Later in the book Lersch summarises the connections between items in the 'endothymic ground' as follows (pp. 301f.):

> Experiences of the endothymic ground reveal the three main themes of human life: existence as a living being, existence as an individual self, and transcending existence. Conations and impulses are characterised by the theme of human life as directedness towards the future, as something to be realised. In feeling-movements we experience their realisation or disappointment as we confront the world from moment to moment. Lastly, enduring moods are states of the endothymic ground in which we continually advance from the past into the present, and against whose background impulses and feeling-movements stand out as occurrences. The theme of being, in the state of perfection or imperfection it has reached, is reflected in them. So the division of endothymic experiences into endothymic moods, movements of feeling and experiences of impulse corresponds to time as we experience it − the trinity of past, present and future.

When Lersch surveys the connection between the endothymic ground and various mental functions not usually included in a list of affective phenomena he pays much attention to the *Gestalt* principle of perception. The basic idea is that all our perceiving results from a kind of 'blind' seeking: we see or hear or feel what we are 'looking for'. This idea is necessary, or at least very plausible, to explain the fact that virtually all our perception is of 'significant wholes', of *objects* and *situations* that 'mean something to us'. Only in exceptional situations, or as the result of special effort, do we simply take in 'impressions' or visual, auditory, or other 'data'. It looks as though 'what' we perceived is what we vaguely and dimly anticipated − from our first entry into the world. Thus the connection between soul and world is from the start a kind of dialogue. These considerations have led some thinkers to talk of *Suchbilder* – literally 'search-images' (as though the baby came into the world armed with a set of 'identikit' pictures of 'food', 'comfort', 'safety' and so on, and 'programmed' to look for the 'answering' objects in the world and to cleave to them) – and of the *Urphantasie* (primary imagination) as innately stocked with such rough 'outlines' and 'schemata'. Lersch sums up as follows: 'The themes of our impulses, our primary imagination and our value-feeling are thus the foundation of world-awareness (as articulated in units of significance), a process in which basic feeling forms the connecting link' since it is the indicator of success or failure (p. 338).

The same sort of analysis is extended to creative imagination as well, in which Lersch sees a 'cognitive anticipation of reality', as when a person suddenly sees a connection between apparently disparate events or patterns of events. No experience can account for this (pp. 374f.):

> It is as though there were laid up in the depths of the soul not only the basic structures of reality, but also of the Possible. Creative imagination is then the process by which the soul raises these out of the unconscious into the clarity of representation . . . The phenomena point once more to relations between soul and world that are of a 'higher ontic order' than what we can actually experience.

All this becomes plausible, and indeed almost necessary, if we interpret the psyche in developmental terms, and see affective phenomena as at the heart of this development. The idea of affective phenomena as being aspects of the dynamics of life thrusting out into the world is a *Leitmotiv* of Polanyi's work.

The place of the Affective in human life can only be fully understood if we compare it with the place of the 'personal superstructure', the seat of thinking and willing. We have seen that the endothymic ground is the 'place' where the world impinges on man, the arena of experience. All fullness, depth, colour and vital *élan* come into our lives at this level. But the endothymic ground is ordained not only to extend 'life' into 'consciousness', but to make possible the spiritual direction of life. Hence we can say that its basic function is to provide humanly relevant 'material' for the personal superstructure to respond to and fashion its life out of. As far as the personal superstructure goes, the task of thought is to clarify and order the contents of the endothymic ground, the task of the will is to select among impulses, choosing the good or the better and rejecting the bad or the worse. Only when *both* layers work together properly can man live a properly human life. This means that the personal superstructure 'is not only able but called to take to itself the themes of all the endothymic movements' (p. 472). Tensions can certainly arise in all this, but the integrated wholeness of experience is not thereby destroyed. The task of integrating and balancing between the two layers is given to man as the task of self-discovery and self-realisation (p. 474).

The Affective and Values

That feelings are in general necessary for evaluation is a common theme in philosophy and psychology. It is clearly expressed by Claparède (1928, p. 159) and by Reid: 'a value situation is one in which we feel about something, and the "value" is what we feel about' (1976, p. 16). Meinong's theory of 'emotional presentation' is a sophisticated working out of the idea (Findlay, 1963, pp. 304ff.). It is strongly emphasised by MacMurray, implicit in Midgley's *Beast and Man* (1978) and almost gets expressed in much other contemporary English philosophy (e.g. Williams, 1965).

However it is also common to find the view that though feeling is *in general* necessary for evaluation, it is not necessary in every case. We have already mentioned Aschenbrenner's view that the vocabulary of moral judgement can be intelligibly used without feeling the corresponding affects, although this could not be the general case. Nevertheless, he holds that 'the capacity for total segregation of affects from judgements' is the surest distinguishing mark 'of a civilized society' (1971, p. 104).

The ability of 'values' to, as it were, 'break free' of feeling is clearly due to their 'consequential' quality, that is, their close connection with 'facts'. Scheler (1973, pp. 12ff.) regards values as 'essences', implying that they just happen to be encountered in actual objects and have some kind of ideal existence on their own. Strasser challenges this view, claiming that values are always experienced either in real or at least in possible objects. Thus, to take an example, we could have no idea of justice at all if we did not find some actual or possible (perhaps imagined) *acts* to be just. But (and here we leave Strasser) we can identify cases of justice or injustice without actually *feeling* anything because there are typical cases of these things that can be identified simply through their factual qualities.

But what can be meant by this? If the arguments of, say, Lersch, Strasser, Langer and Reid are correct, there can be no experience which is not a case of feeling. Certainly we can identify cases of injustice in the sense that we can argue: 'if three men agree to do the pools jointly and to share their winnings equally, then it will be unjust if one of the men takes more than his share' (although one might insist here, too, that, if this argument is really to *mean* anything to us, we must somehow re-live the moral experiences of injustice on which it ultimately depends, or 'represent' them to ourselves in some way), but if we are to *experience* a case of injustice then we shall have to apprehend it at the level of feeling-awareness, or in the endothymic ground. In that sense, then, our feeling of the value is no different from our feeling of the persons involved in the transaction, or the actual deeds or words that constituted it. 'Feeling' here simply means 'apprehension' – the dim and fleeting though often poignant way in which the world first impinges on us; though it is of course true that such apprehension necessarily involves awareness of some kind of feeling-quality. We are aware of things 'feeling' in this way or that. In this sense the feeling of value is inextricably bound up with grasping an aspect of reality.

But this is clearly not what is usually meant when it is said that facts are simply apprehended, whereas 'values' are felt. There is clearly a difference between taking in facts and taking in values. The experience of value is the experience of being *moved*, but the experience of fact – of indifferent fact – is not. Lersch gives us a clue in his analysis of feeling-movements. A component of these experiences is an element of impulse that points to an appropriate response to the value that has moved us (1954, p. 190). Edith Stein distinguishes between the act of grasping the value (feeling it) and the appropriate feeling-*response* to it (1970, p. 191). She points out that both elements need each other. There can be no proper response without a proper grasp, no adequate grasp without adequate response.

Nevertheless, it does seem that Strasser is right to insist that, at the level of feeling, it is not that we experience 'facts' in one way, 'values' in another, but that we experience all objects and situations as moving us, as significant to us, in various ways and to various degrees, verging perhaps on zero (1977, p. 132). Even our value-*responses*, that is, are directed to the bearers of value (the valuable or significant objects or situations) rather than to the values themselves. The separation of things into 'facts' and 'factual characteristics' on the one hand and 'values' or 'value-qualities' on the other thus only occurs at the level of conceptual thought. However, it is also true that this separation is justified by the fact that the 'echo of feeling' that objects and situations may leave may enable us to recognise them again when we cannot say anything else about them. In retrospect, that is, we can indirectly distinguish value aspects from factual ones (p. 133).

Lersch also points to the difference between 'intellectual' and 'spiritual' thinking. Both start from experience and strive to fashion 'a surveyable, ordered and coherent horizon of reality' (by 'horizon' he means something like 'environment'), but, whereas intellectual thought aims to produce 'a horizon of objects and states of affairs with which we reckon and calculate' (compare Sartre's stress on instrumentality and

MacMurray's attack on it), spiritual thought aims for 'a horizon of meaningful objects that can be conceptually determined and related to each other' (Lersch, 1954, p. 397). Sartre, of course, calls this arbitrary – a deliberate, willed drop into the magical, or at least, so it seems, a willing consent to experience the world in magical terms that seems in the end a shameful indulgence. But Lersch is the better phenomenologist here. 'In all this the idea' (ideas include 'values' as well as 'essences') 'exercises a liberating and directive power on the knower, and therein shows itself to be living and quickening in a manner that has no parallel in the sphere of intellectual thought' (ibid., p. 398). It is the difference between a classification that imposes itself on us as significant, and one that we find it convenient or useful to impose.

In other words, although values are in a sense an abstraction from experience, and result from directing one's thinking in one way rather than another, the procedure is justified by its results: man's striving for meaning, and indeed for what is meaningful in itself, is thereby fulfilled – despite the fact, it must be acknowledged, that there is far less agreement between people about values than about facts in our deeply technological age. But it should also be clear that 'value-free' facts are every bit as much of an abstraction as values themselves, since they too can only be established by directing our thinking in one way rather than another, and this procedure is also justified simply by its results. For man also strives for mastery and control of his world, and thus his 'intellectual thought' also fulfils one of the great themes of his conations.

But, to return to the starting-point of this section, if evaluation is conceived of as a pure exercise of thinking, the application of general principles to cases firmly grasped under concepts, then it can certainly be carried out without feeling. But, in the first place, the principles must ultimately be derived from experience – which means that they must be based on something felt and feelingly responded to. Unless individuals constantly return to experience, and feel the underlying realities for themselves, their evaluations (moral or aesthetic judgements, and so on) will become lifeless and meaningless after a time, since man is not only a thinker but also a 'feeler', and he needs to act with the whole of himself. Secondly, by far the majority of cases to be evaluated in ordinary life are not so easily grasped under concepts as the abstract examples of moral philosophers suggest. There will, of necessity, have to be a recourse to experience, to confrontation with the individual case, where it will frequently be found that the really difficult thing is to choose between rival descriptions (applications of concepts). Was such and such an act an act of justice (and therefore good) or of heartless cruelty (and therefore bad)? No principle can guarantee to tell us. 'Feeling' is essential, because it is all that we have to go on. We have to feel and respond to the case in all its particularity (Bantock, 1967, p. 73, gives a good example). We have also, of course, to think about the case, to bring it under concepts and principles, but then again the test of whether we have done *that* properly is that it feels right. Both thinking and feeling are necessary for all but the most simple and uncomplicated cases. To imagine we can do without either is to dehumanise ourselves.

The Structure of Feeling

In his book *Education in Religion and the Emotions* John Wilson writes (1971, pp. 90f.):

> To such general questions as 'what sort of things ought to be desired or feared (pitied, loved, etc.)?' we can return no answer that is of any permanent value to the educator. For either we shall give a purely conceptual answer (e.g. 'desirable things', or 'dangerous things', 'pitiable things', etc.), which is of no practical use: or else we shall indulge in empirical generalizations, the truth of which is contingent upon (a) particular, and (b) mutable, empirical facts.

The last point Wilson makes here is a reference to his belief that whatever structure of 'interests' human beings in general, or particular groups of human beings, may happen to have, 'geneticists or other scientists' can always change them. Hence there is no point in talking about 'the structure of feeling' at all. Instead philosophers of education should elucidate 'general principles of rationality for practical living', basing their thought rather on the essence of 'rational creature', which is, he implies, eternal, than on the structure of human feeling, which is changeable, if not changing (pp. 91f.).

In contrast to Wilson, Mary Midgley powerfully argues in *Beast and Man* (1978) that man has a nature 'like any other species', and that moral philosophy and, presumably, philosophy of education must base its recommendations on the basic structure of wants and preferences which constitutes this nature. Indeed, reason *includes* the idea of a structure of wants and preferences (cf. MacMurray). Hence the only way to talk rationally about what ought to be desired, feared, and so on, is to find out what we really and permanently want and prefer with the whole of ourselves. This notion of 'deep' or 'real' wants as opposed to superficial, fleeting and momentarily excited wants and feelings is also found in Felix Krueger (1928, pp. 105f.). He calls genuine wants and so on 'structurally conditioned' but, unlike Midgley, acknowledges that structurally conditioned feelings conflict, implying that such conflict reflects a split in our nature.

In a work of this modest length I cannot further argue the importance of the structure of feeling. I have tried to show that all talk of 'rationality' ultimately leads us back to it. The present task is to show that some account can be given of it. For this we must turn once again to Lersch, since Midgley does not herself investigate it — though she certainly drops a good many hints as to what it may or may not contain. But in response to Wilson's conviction that it is not the business of the philosopher to talk about such 'particular' and 'mutable' things as the 'structure of human feelings' we may say this: as to the particularity, people — and peoples — do of course show great variations, but at the same time they show great similarities, and men and women can eventually find themselves to some degree at home with any group of human beings however alien they may continue to find them in some respects. The acid test, perhaps, is their ability to 'enter into' the acts of other people. *Nil humanum a me alienum puto.* If a man can truthfully say that he considers nothing human to be alien to him, then there must be a universal *structure* of feeling, however different the forms in which it has found expression may be. As to the 'mutability' of human nature, this is a mere assumption. There is no doubt that we could destroy ourselves, but the idea of 'changing our nature' — of 're-creating' ourselves as beings with a different set of fundamental needs, wants and preferences — seems to me to be incoherent (see also Dunlop, 1982, pp. 217–21). And I also take it that philosophy is a human activity for humans, not the activity of some mythical 'genus' of 'rational beings'. So much for Wilson's disclaimers. The question of the structure of human feeling is far too important to be simply ignored.

Quite a few psychologists offer accounts of the structure of feeling, or of emotion, or of appetition. But one can never be quite sure how comprehensive they are supposed to be, and there is often the lurking suspicion that the research methods adopted have artificially restricted the range of material to the more 'basic','primitive', or conspicuously expressed phenomena. But Lersch's account is firmly based within a complete psychological-philosophical account of man. Of all the accounts I have seen it is much the most interesting and comprehensive. There will be no time to discuss it. But I offer it here in summary form as the best example I know of an essential aspect of the study of man.

(A) Impulses

(Lersch lists these in the order in which they develop)

(1) Impulses to experience the 'vitality' of existence, in which one feels the dynamism and flow of life as it reaches its goal:
    (a) drive to be active, to experience oneself as *moving* oneself;
    (b) drive to become aware of oneself, to experience one's inner states:
        (i) striving for enjoyment (mental or physical),

    (ii) libido (sex),

    (iii) drive to have experiences (of any kind).

(2) Impulses of existence as an individual self:

    (a) drive for self-maintenance and self-preservation;

    (b) 'egoism' – drive to possess things, to exploit the environment for one's own use;

    (c) will to power;

    (d) drive for social recognition;

    (e) drive for retribution;

    (f) drive for value in one's own eyes.

(3) Impulses of transcending existence, in which we hear a call to go out beyond ourselves:

    (a) drives directed towards the social world:

        (i) drive for shared life, for company,

        (ii) drive to take a responsible share in community life;

    (b) drive to contribute to the common stock of values;

    (c) drive to take a cognitive interest in things;

    (d) drive to take a loving interest in eternal reality itself, ideals, etc.;

    (e) drive to experience values as binding on oneself (to answer the call of values in 'impersonal' ways);

    (f) drive to struggle free of finitude and associate oneself with the absolute, associated with religion, art and philosophy.

(B) Movements of Feeling

(likewise to be thought of in developmental sequence; many of these are signs of the *frustration* of corresponding impulses)

(1) Feeling-movements of existence as a living being (of pre-individual existence):

    (a) pain (mental and physical);

    (b) pleasure (fulfils the theme of existence at this level), enjoyment (life as more intense);

    (c) boredom;

    (d) satiety, aversion;

    (e) disgust, loathing;

    (f) amusement, vexation (pleasure in functioning, frustration);

    (g) joy and sadness (enrichment and impoverishment of existence);

    (h) delight and horror (ecstatic embracement of life, threat to life itself).

(2) Feeling-movements of existence as an individual self:

    (a) feeling-movements of self-preservation:

        (i) fright,

        (ii) agitation,

      (iii) rage,
      (iv) fear,
      (v) trust and mistrust;
  (b) feeling-movements of egoism, power-striving and the drive for social recognition:
      (i) content and discontent (relate to all three impulses),
      (ii) envy (relates to egoism),
      (iii) jealousy,
      (iv) triumph and defeat,
      (v) feeling flattered or hurt;
  (c) feeling-movements of the retributive drive:
      (i) feeling of 'satisfaction',
      (ii) joy in another's hurt (*Schadenfreude*),
      (iii) gratitude;
  (d) feeling-movements of the striving for self-worth:
      (i) feelings of inferiority and shame,
      (ii) self-respect, self-contempt, remorse.
(3) Feeling-movements of transcending existence:
  (a) social feeling-movements:
      (i) feeling-movements of social existence –
        1 sympathy and antipathy
        2 respect and contempt
        3 reverence and scorn,
      (ii) feeling-movements of social concern –
        1 fellow-feeling
        2 love (for the individual person)
        3 erotic and neighbour-love
        4 hate;
  (b) feeling-movements of creative and cognitive participation:
      (i) joy in creation,
      (ii) 'noetic' feelings – amazement, wonder, doubt, conviction;
  (c) feeling-movements of loving and obligatory participation:
      (i) love (for what has meaning, for what is good),
      (ii) 'normative' feelings – feelings of duty and justice, the sense of obligation, anger and indignation (at breaches of the moral order);
  (d) feeling-movements of participation in a higher sphere of existence:
      (i) artistic emotions (art is here interpreted as the search for absolutes through sensual appearances),
      (ii) metaphysical feelings, philosophical wonder, awe,
      (iii) religious emotion and religious awe.

(C) 'Heart' and 'Conscience'

Lersch appends to his long analysis of feeling-movements a short discussion of 'heart' and 'conscience', which especially characterise the sphere of transcendence. 'Heart' is not just concerned with interpersonal life, but with anything to which one feels bound or committed, in which one feels and responds to value. In feeling-movements of the heart we feel the 'meaning-values' of the world (if something has 'meaning-value' it has significance in itself), and thus fulfil the third great theme of our conative life. In 'conscience' all that we experience as binding in the movements of the heart is related to our action. It is closely bound up with the feeling of responsibility for the world, our own life and our own self. Remorse is a feeling-movement of conscience, and all its movements also connect with the theme of self-worth. Thus as a sphere of feeling conscience belongs where the theme of being an individual self passes over into that of transcending oneself. It is here that the 'person', as opposed to the individual, constitutes itself.

(D) 'Feelings of Fate'

But there is another category of feeling-movement which corresponds to the most general theme of impulses − the future. Lersch calls these 'feelings of fate' (*Schicksal*), or feelings related in the most general sense to one's existence in time. They arise from the various ways in which impulses may be experienced as fulfilled or not yet fulfilled. They are:

(1) expectation, going with patience and impatience,
(2) surprise, startle, consternation (pleasant or unpleasant),
(3) hope, connected with disappointment,
(4) apprehension and concern,
(5) resignation,
(6) despair.

(E) Affective States of the Endothymic Ground (including moods)

(1) Life-feeling:
   (*a*) bodily feeling-states: comfort and discomfort, cold and heat, hunger, thirst, satiety, tiredness, sleepiness, freshness, sickness, feeling ill, feeling of bodily strength and weakness, bodily tension and relaxation, restlessness and calm, lasting pain;
   (*b*) life-moods:
      (i) serenity,
      (ii) cheerfulness,
      (iii) melancholy,
      (iv) discontent
      (equanimity is analysed as stability of life-mood);
   (*c*) excited and dramatic forms of life-feeling:
      (i) anguish − life-anguish, existential anguish, inner anguish,
      (ii) ecstasy.
(2) Self-feeling:
   (*a*) Feeling of one's own power, 'self-confidence';

(b) feeling of self-worth (centred either in others' evaluations, or one's own);

(c) feeling of inferiority (gives rise to sentimentality);

(d) content and discontent.

(3) World-feeling:

    (a) gravity, seriousness;

    (b) optimism and pessimism;

    (c) nihilism;

    (d) humour.

It must be pointed out that nearly every one of these items that I have in most cases barely listed is accompanied by an incisive and graphic analysis that would do much, if there were space to reproduce it, to offset the frequently approximate nature of my translation. But my aim in presenting this analsis of the structure of feeling has been to give some idea of how it can be done.

In the case of the first two lists – impulses and feeling-movements – it will be noted that the items are listed in developmental order. The suggestion is that a person who is affectively fully developed will be capable of experiencing the full gamut of both conations and feelings, some as a matter of course, others only as a result of contingencies. In addition, his impulses and feelings will themselves indicate their proper objects. Thus they will be 'rational', thanks to the element of 'pre-cognition' contained in them, provided the subject 'rules' himself justly.

It should be noted once more that Lersch sees a clash, possibly a virtually necessary clash, between existence as an individual self and transcending existence. Thus, although a person who *could not feel* envy, jealousy, *Schadenfreude,* or the desire for revenge would be affectively undeveloped, the developed person will also feel conations and feelings that require him to transcend them in forms of love and forgiveness. But there is no suggestion that there is some 'ideal' resolution to which all can resort. It is, we might say, for each person to cope with the 'split' in himself as best he may, though normally he will accept the help of a social or religious ethos – that is, a particular and historically conditioned set of principles of preference between conations.

The Expression of Feeling and Emotion

In a short section on the place of the body (above, pp. 37–40) I emphasised the lack of success psychologists have had in unambiguously correlating particular emotions with particular bodily symptoms. This is surprising when we recall how easy it is to 'read' other people's feelings in ordinary life. But it should not be difficult to see how different these operations are. In the first case psychologists deliberately isolate 'bodily symptoms' from the experienced totality of the subjects observed, and try to establish empirical links between such 'symptoms' and the emotions or feelings the subjects say they are experiencing. But in ordinary life we do not normally take things as 'symptoms' at all, but perceive feelings immediately in their physical manifestations: joy in laughter, sorrow and pain in tears, shame in blushing, the tenor of thoughts in the sound of words (Scheler, 1954, p. 260; Stein, 1970, p. 71). The notion of symptoms only arises when this immediate feeling-awareness is somehow checked, as when there is some discrepancy between a person's feelings now, as 'seen', and those we expected on the basis of the situation or our previous knowledge of him, or when we suspect some kind of hypocrisy or insincerity or derangement. But, as Scheler points out (1954, pp. 261f.), these very 'checks' and 'suspicions' actually *presuppose* direct perception of feeling.

Scheler argues that we first know persons as 'animate bodies', in which there is complete interpenetration of 'inner' and 'outer'. The splitting of the two spheres from each other is a deliberate and subsequent act (ibid., p. 218). He also claims that 'the world' is first given to infants – and still is, predominantly, to some 'primitives' – as 'one vast field of expression' (everything is animate to them), and that hence our pre-scientific knowledge of nature is based on the essentially 'expressive aspect of living organisms'. For it is an extraordinary fact that we can understand some of what animals are feeling (just as they are aware of some of our feelings) and that very young children have an impressive knowledge of their parents' feelings – within the range of their own emotional development (Midgley, 1978, p. 311).

'Expression' is thus a fundamental aspect of life. Soul and body interpenetrate, inner state is reflected in outward appearance just as the outer is appropriated by the inner. Hence, at the level of feeling-awareness, knowledge of other people's feelings is direct and immediate. We simply 'take in at a glance' (sometimes erroneously) what others are feeling. Scheler talks of a universal 'mime, pantomime and grammar of expression' which underlies all particular *languages* of expression (involving, say, the wagging of tails or the rubbing of noses; 1954, p. 11). At this level of human life expression is a natural phenomenon, an eloquent testimony to man's oneness with nature.

But man's own nature is such that he can distance himself from himself, survey his body and soul (or parts of them) and create the categories of *'inner* life' and *'outward* expression'. 'Expression' can now be interpreted as an 'activity' (Benson, 1967, p. 336), even one that is 'rule-governed' (William Alston, as quoted in Benson, ibid.). It can be said to be inspired by the 'purposes' of 'communication' with others (Schrag, 1973, p. 31), or performed with the 'intention' of finding out what one is really feeling (Benson, 1967, p. 340). Man can inhibit expression, or exaggerate it, or use it to pretend he is feeling something he thinks he ought to feel but cannot. But inhibited feelings, those, that is, that are repeatedly denied expression, tend to disappear from consciousness after a time – perhaps to exercise a malign influence on the psyche from the depths of 'the unconscious'. Scheler points out that, in general, we have most knowledge of our mental states when they find some kind of expression in gesture, language, or movement, or at least when we experience them as tending towards such bodily form. This should be clear when we recall the 'obscurity' and 'fleetingness' of consciousness at the level of feeling-awareness. Bodily expression performs the same sort of role as conceptual grasp in 'fixing' and 'solidifying' the deliverances of experience. Thus, if we would know ourselves, it is important not to repress our feelings too strongly. Edith Stein also points out how we experience forms of expression (including verbal forms) as 'terminations' of our feelings. Feelings press for some kind of completion (another indication of the essentially dynamic nature of the Affective) and prescribe not only secondary 'volitions' or 'conations' (towards 'instrumental' activity), but also appropriate forms of expression (Stein, 1970, p. 48). These, she argues, need not *actually* be bodily; the *imagined* carrying-out of the appropriate volition in the appropriate way may be enough. Alternatively feelings can 'terminate' in reflection on the situation. Such 'reflection' need not weaken the life of feeling in general (presumably because in it we acknowledge it, and take up a stance towards it; ibid., p. 49). But a consideration of the underlying 'dynamics' should make us see that although 'conventional' expressive elements can, and indeed are bound (such is human nature) to take over from natural elements to a certain extent, this process of substitution must have its limits. Once conventional expressions of feeling (including shaking hands, 'thumbs-up' signs, and so on) can no longer be *experienced* as satisfactory 'terminations' of feeling, then the feelings in question, denied proper expression, will either gradually disappear – to the detriment, indeed crippling, of our lives as wholes – or 'go underground' (perhaps to wreak havoc from there), or perhaps lead to 'outbursts' and 'explosions' of emotion proper, when we lose or surrender all control of ourselves. Schrag clearly puts the case for the logical priority of 'natural' over 'conventional' forms of expression, at the same time arguing that both are needed (1973, pp. 33ff). But in fact the distinction between nature and convention is exceedingly obscure in itself (Dunlop, 1982, pp. 217–21).

A note on the expressiveness of nature and art. Aestheticians have long been exercised over the phenomenon of 'gloomy' landscapes and 'joyful' music (see, for example, Baensch, 1923–4, and Hepburn, 1965). As lovers of natural scenery and art most of us feel inclined to say that we experience qualities of gloominess, joy, and so on, *in* the objects of our appreciation. But reflective thought seems on the other hand to forbid this. For how could essentially 'psychic' or 'mental' states be properties of objects that had no consciousness?

However, Lersch classifies 'cheerfulness' and 'melancholy' as 'life-feelings', as states of pre-individual life. At this lowest level of our experience there is no differentiation between subject and object; we are simply aware of a 'quality' of the 'life' that we share with what surrounds us. But landscapes and works of art are themselves phenomena of life, either literally, in the vegetation that does so much to give landscape its quality, or metaphorically, in the 'living form' of art and the 'sculptural' and formal aspects of landscape (see Langer, 1967, Vol. I, ch. 7). It seems, then, that the 'gloominess' and the 'joy' mentioned above may be best understood as qualities of *life* (at the pre-individual level), qualities that we may discern either in ourselves, or in others, or in anything else in which there is 'life', provided that we 'sink' to the requisite level of experience and remain there long enough to allow ourselves to be impinged on.

If we then ask whether these qualities are 'really' in the landscapes, works of art, and so on, we have first to make clear which qualities are in question (there is no question of 'directed feelings' in the above examples), and then ascertain which level of consciousness we are talking about. Questions about the ultimate metaphysical status of the deliverances of the levels are beyond the scope of this book.

Authentic and Inauthentic Feeling

The question of authenticity in feeling is of great importance in human life, and presents some difficult pedagogical problems.

Findlay talks about 'unserious wants' (1961, pp. 165f.). These are not necessarily not *felt*, in the sense in which feeling 'involves a peculiar intensification of experience', but they have a 'parasitic, shallowly rooted, therefore unsustainable character'. They 'prolong patterns impinging relatively externally on the conscious person – as when we enter into other people's wants, or desire to impress them with our sympathy'. They are 'rootless in the personality', finding their cognitive analogues in unserious belief.

Lersch likewise insists that inauthentic feeling is to be distinguished from hypocrisy, insincerity and untruthfulness. There is absolutely no element of intent to deceive in it. As Alexander Pfänder puts it, the inauthentic person does not just imitate the outward forms of expression in order to conceal something (though of course *some* people do this). He really does *feel* things, but he does it inauthentically (Pfänder, 1922, pp. 58–64). Lersch adds that the trouble with the inauthentic person is that he has allowed himself to 'intervene in [his] own inwardness'. Inauthentic feelings are thus somewhere between authentic or genuine and merely feigned feelings. When a man wants to be sad about someone's death and tries hard to be so his feelings may be 'empty, hollow, without substance', not welling up from the depths as genuine feelings would.

Inauthentic feelings, continues Lersch, are not experienced by others as *expressions* of feeling. It is rather as though the 'appearances' of grief are produced 'from without'. There is an absence of the 'particular psychic substance' needed for genuine grief, which wells creatively up from the depths, connecting the expressive physiognomy of grief with the life-ground. Inauthenticity must also be distinguished from the case where a person cannot adequately *express* his genuine feelings because of some kind of inhibition or block. The category of inauthenticity covers all other affective and other kinds of mental phenomena.

Lersch suggests several causes of inauthenticity: conformity to expectations, suggestive power of one's milieu, striving for recognition, hunger for certain experiences of which one is incapable. Clearly many of the feelings of children and young people are inauthentic. The educational challenge is to teach them in such a way that 'external form and inner experience keep pace with one another'. But in many highly educated people it is extremely hard to distinguish authentic from inauthentic feeling. The split between 'inner' and 'outer' is extremely well disguised. But inauthenticity is a constant danger for all of us, especially in situations (perhaps at work, or in social life) we cannot live up to. Inauthentic thinking is a special temptation for the intellectual.

Why is inauthenticity necessarily bad – or, at any rate, a *danger*? Because, in losing touch with the depths or heart of oneself, one loses the sense of meaning in life and cuts oneself off from one's own source of creative growth and renewal within. The authentic man is 'at one with himself'. He lives out of his own 'soul-substance'. His 'inner' and 'outer' interpenetrate, as in organic growth. He is the 'natural' man. But thanks to his power of thought and will man can desert his own nature. He can lose touch with his feelings, his heart, his depths, the source of life in him. Thus inauthenticity is a falling away from the organic, from life, from integrated existence. It sets in with the emergence of self-consciousness, which means that man ceases to live automatically from his centre, since he can now reject whole sides of himself and model himself on others.

All this, Lersch concludes, points to the vital importance of the unconscious, where everything in man has its origins. All authentic human achievements are produced by following 'rules' that are *not known* to consciousness (as Polanyi puts it, one always knows more than one can say). But consciousness need not lead to inauthenticity. It is man's task and vocation to be true to himself and not succumb to it.

This account of Lersch's (1954, pp. 503–27) is quite free from the anti-bourgeois bias of Heidegger (see his account of *das Man* in *Being and Time*). There can be no doubt that inauthentic feeling is extremely common. The resulting educational problem is one of the most urgent problems confronting teachers today. The phenomenon, widely acknowledged in practice if seldom analysed (though see Bonnett, 1978), points once more to the dynamic and developmental picture of man I have constantly emphasised in these pages. No doubt the sort of stress on 'logical' development to be found in the works of some educational philosophers (see above all Hirst and Peters, 1970, ch. 3) can *in practice* be combined with this sort of view, but on the face of it they are distinct, and it is hard to think of anything more likely to lead to inauthentic, and thus in the end anti-human, thought, feeling and choice than the doctrine that none of this can count as 'rational' or 'educated' unless it results from the application of public and social criteria that are simply imposed on the self. But this flight from nature as the place of error, deformity and breakdown is self-defeating, since reasoning is an activity of man, the living organism. Authenticity certainly entails the possibility of failure. But it is better to be authentically human and possibly wrong than strive inauthentically for conformity and the illusion of certainty.

Some Enemies and Dangers of Feeling

Nothing appears to diminish the significance of thymic [Affective] experience as much as the technicizing of human existence. In the measure in which it advances, experiences of attraction and of impulse become unimportant, and, on the contrary, insights into relations of positing goals and purposes and of attaining them become standard. Feeling becomes superfluous; indeed, it operates in a disordering and disturbing manner. (Strasser, 1977, p. 251)

Hence the call for life to be governed by 'skills and routines', instead of by real feeling-responses to situations, and of the pressure to 'mak[e] out of a well developed automatism the most valuable instrument of our personality'. In a world that worships machines and machine-like efficiency men become mechanical themselves. To the technical thinker feeling becomes 'merely subjective'.

There are three ways in particular in which the spread of technical attitudes threatens feeling:

(1) The main theme of technology – the control and mastery of nature – makes it harder for people to see themselves as *part* of nature,

and thus to take their *own* nature seriously. The very success of technology encourages man to think that he can 're-make' himself. This is dangerous utopian nonsense, as I have argued elsewhere (Dunlop, 1982, pp. 217–21). But in rejecting the idea of a 'given' nature man also rejects the idea of a given stock of impulses and feelings, which must be developed, properly directed and fitted together harmoniously (as far as this is possible). Feeling itself is thus taken less seriously.

(2) The technological attitude replaces trust in one's own experience, or in the traditional wisdom of family, clan, culture and the human race, with reliance on books, manuals, instruction sheets, the 'authoritative' pronouncements of experts. Thus men come to mistrust their feelings as a reliable guide to life and come gradually to live in a second-hand world, one that has been classified, categorised and 'evaluated' for them by total strangers.

(3) Impulses and feelings of transcending experience (to use Lersch's term) are especially vulnerable. Technology does not and cannot destroy all feeling and impulse. But because the impulses served by technology are almost entirely confined to those of living existence and individual existence these two spheres of the affective life (or parts of them) gain much more prominence and, in so far as the themes of transcending existence (spiritual or 'meaning' values) are taken account of at all, they are re-interpreted or 'reduced' to those of the two lower levels of value (truth as 'useful belief', or 'socially approved belief', and so on). This transference of emphasis is made more likely by the fact that we tend to experience the themes of transcendence as in competition with the themes of living and individual existence.

But we can go further. In turning away from transcending themes or, alternatively, in experiencing them largely in terms of the themes of individual existence – as when individual scholars pursue their researches almost wholly to answer the drive for power or social recognition – man mutilates himself. For he is incomplete without transcendent objects. His transcending impulses continue to well up from the unconscious layers of his psyche, but because they are denied 'termination' there is no answering feeling and they eventually atrophy. But he also becomes less able to feel, his impulses become less lively, at the lower levels of affectivity. For the objects of transcending experiences are themselves life-giving: beauty refreshes us, company invigorates us, in selfless love we get back far more than we give. Hence the technological attitude not only tends to cut one off from higher values; it also makes life and feeling less satisfying at the lower levels.

The only way to combat these life-denying tendencies of technical attitudes is to reinstate feeling, and especially transcending feelings, in the life of man. It would be absurd to reject technology itself; the technical approach is just as human as some of the non-technical approaches, even if, in a certain sense, it is 'lower' (though more urgent) than they. Nor would it make sense to restrict the spread of technical attitudes artificially, through political control. For this could only be done through the exercise of power, which is one of the main impulses behind modern technology. The technological attitude can only be counteracted through exhibiting the attractiveness of 'wholeness', of a life in which technical-instrumental and spiritual themes are properly balanced. If the over-technicised life leads to deadness and emptiness (cf. Forster, 1954), the rejection of the technical virtues (efficiency, rule-following, careful reckoning and calculation, refusal to be distracted from the end, and so on) can lead to injustice, improvidence and 'parasitism'.

Some people think one can counteract the dangers of technology, and the related 'intellectualism', by an exaggerated hostility to the intellect. The slogan 'trust your feelings' becomes the complete guide to life. If this is interpreted as compatible with 'trust thinking', and all other mental activities, no harm will result. The good life entails trust in all human capacities. But all too often it implies a refusal to think, and drags its devotees down to the level of base self-indulgence. The fact is that 'trust your feelings' frequently means 'trust the first impulse that comes into your head', and ignores the fact that not all impulses come from deep within us. Findlay's description of 'unserious wants' may be recalled here (p. 80 above). 'Trust your feelings' is all too often an encouragement to inauthenticity.

Another way in which the evils of technicism and intellectualism are sometimes coped with is the resort to sentimentality. Tanner sees the essence of this as 'render [ing one] self more passive' (1976–7, p. 134). In Lersch's terms, one lets the personal superstructure 'idle' or go out of action. The 'self' becomes a mere passive 'experiencer', refusing from time to time to intervene in its own mental economy and relishing the experience of being 'swept away'. Tanner sees two broad categories of sentimentalist: 'those who let life do what it will with them, and languish in more or less exquisite torment; and those who seize every opportunity for "drinking life to the dregs", etc.'. Clearly both involve a failure in thinking, and a refusal to face up to the realities and responsibilities of the human condition.

Perhaps the most important because most insidious danger in the life of feeling is passion – or rather, misdirected passion. Passion could perhaps have been listed above as a separate affective phenomenon, but it is not purely affective, so it seemed best to reserve it for discussion at this point. Strasser's analysis is the most illuminating one I know.

He begins his treatment with a discussion of what is translated as 'basic transcending comportment'. 'If man justly carries the name *animal religiosum,* this means that, according to his deepest nature, he anticipates the completion of his existence by a transcendent Being'. The pattern of man's development and the pattern of his stratified being thus both 'point' to some ideal possibility beyond the given world that will complete his existence and finally satisfy him. Nevertheless, 'Transcendence is set as a task for man'; no blue-print of this being, or of the way he has to take to find it, is 'written in' to human nature. Nor can he get any guarantee that he has chosen or is choosing right from other men. He is faced with the task of finding his completion alone (1977, pp. 290f.).

Man is also a being of 'metaphysical vulnerability'. It is not only true that he may fail in any particular thing he does. He knows that at the end of his days he may look back on his life as a *total* failure. He is thus threatened with total meaninglessness. So transcendence is given to him as 'the no-longer-worldly focus of all meaning and value', as the total meaning of his acts. In some dim recess of feeling man is pre-cognitively aware of something that answers this tremendous metaphysical need. But because of the difficulty of his task he is constantly tempted to 'absolutize' some region of value that has already brought satisfaction and treat it as though it could satisfy him absolutely. 'In this way pleasure, cruelty, power, avarice, and so forth, become forms of transcending experience.' As such they have great organising power in his life, giving it a recognisable concentrated directedness (ibid., pp. 292f.).

Transcending experience need not itself be passionate, since it can also be calm, playful, contemplative, or dogmatic. But passion also absolutises 'a determinate value'. In addition, for talk of passion to be in place, there must also be a 'heightened susceptibility and capacity for abandonment' to what is valuable (p. 294). For passion entails being overpowered or mastered. The passionate man is so primed that as soon as he encounters what seems to him to be 'the meaningful as such' (the absolutely valuable) he can only respond with total abandon. He lets himself be completely gripped and held.

Thus passion too has great organising power. The passionate man's behaviour is marked by 'consistency, perseverance, composure and awareness of goal . . . He is disciplined in many respects in order to dedicate himself all the more unreservedly to a single thing.' Passion concentrates and narrows human being. It is also of an ethical nature, and thus brings about an enhancement of powers. Man hears a call to reach out beyond himself and grasp the Absolute, though he can only do so through 'concrete bearers of the value in question . . . persons, human societies, things, but also thought-creations and transcendent realities' (p. 296).

As was the case with 'transcending comportment', man can thus miss his way and 'enclose [s] himself in a finite region of value and meaning'. Indeed, the passionate man's Absolute can be a great deal more limited and confined than that of non-passionate men. Hence he often finds

85

himself in conflict both with others and with himself. Is passion then condemned to absurdity, to metaphysical illusion? Strasser answers this question obscurely, but the general tenor of his answer is this: all human striving has some dim and obscure 'pre-cognition' of its goal. Any other assumption is unintelligible. For how could man, a living being, experience a need that could not be satisfied? Certainly there are delusions and errors. But these must be seen as deviations from the path; the path itself cannot be illusory.

Thus 'the passionate mode of basic comportment can be a suitable value-response to the actual call of Transcendence' (there can also be mystical-ascetic, contemplative and speculative answers; p. 299). Nevertheless, there is also an 'antinomy' even here, since man can only respond to transcendence through the mediation of 'worldly signs, events, persons, communities and activities'. Man can never grasp the nature of this Absolute value and Absolute meaning; he can only know it as a direction whence he hears his call. Hence religious passion is 'foolishness' to the non-believer – and, indeed, sometimes to the believer too unless he dedicates himself to the Absolute he has sensed with all the concentration and power of which he is capable. Finally, then, this sort of passion is justified precisely because its implicit goal is not clear and man needs help to reach it. For man has to struggle up towards transcendence amid all the confusing distractions of bodily involvement and rootedness in feeling. 'In the mode of passionate concentration he avoids the danger of dissipation and superficiality' (p. 301).

Our attitude to passion will thus clearly depend on whether we believe there exists an adequate object for it. There is no doubt that passionate men have produced some of the greatest of human goods; equally, there is no doubt that other such men have contributed enormously to human misery. The dangers and risks of the life of feeling are nowhere more apparent than here. But if we believe, with Strasser, Lersch, MacMurray and others, that all true goals for man are already somehow indicated in the structure of human feeling, then the answer seems clear. The passionate child must not be weaned from this way of comporting himself in the world, or taught that these phenomena are really a sign of the 'absurdity' of the universe. He must be shown how to find for himself the one true and fully adequate object of passion, which the religious believer calls God.

5

Educating the Emotions

R. S. Peters asserts that 'the education of the emotions is inescapably a moral matter' (1970, p. 182). It should be clear by now that I see things differently. The reason why it is *not* largely a thematically moral matter is that it is a matter of development. The idea of development implies that the *ends* of the process are somehow present 'in germ', or 'implicitly', or 'potentially', at the very beginning of the process. In our case I have argued that we should see the 'structure of human feeling' (which largely constitutes human nature) as implicitly 'aimed at' or 'groped towards' from the beginning of an infant's life. If it is the task of 'the education of the emotions' to encourage the growth of this structure then it cannot be 'inescapably a moral matter' for, if it were, we should have to say that the structure aimed at is arrived at through a series of thematically moral choices (as when we choose between good and evil, virtue and vice, the lesser of two evils or the greater of two goods, and so on), rather than implicit in human life itself.

It might, of course, be thought that if the education of the emotions were merely a matter of development it would proceed under its own momentum, and not require the help or intervention of teachers. There are two main reasons why this conclusion is not justified. First, all living things need an appropriate *environment* in which to develop. In the case of human beings an essential part of this environment is the presence of other human beings who not only attend to them, meeting their physical needs, but interact with them. For man is an essentially *social* being. Secondly, the 'structure of human feeling' is a largely 'open', formless and unfixed thing. The human person strives for self-preservation, to take an example. But what the actual dangers are, and how they are to be warded off, depends, among other things, on what part of the world he is born into and how his people have coped with it. It is thus his social group, his 'society', that fills in the details for him. The same goes for transcending conations. Formally speaking, a person needs objects to be responsible for, values to pursue on behalf of his group, questions to interest him, and so on. His 'culture' tells him where to look. It is possible that in the case of some of the higher drives, exceptionally gifted individuals would themselves discover appropriate objects for their unfolding conations. Indeed the 'genius' is the man who does precisely this, in that (though he may start from them) he goes beyond the common stock of tried solutions. But, by and large, the human person relies on the accumulated experience of his forebears. His 'culture', 'subculture', and so on, provide him with more or less appropriate 'forms' through which his developing conations and feelings may achieve satisfaction. Emotional development thus cannot be left to the individual himself. (On this general topic, see Midgley, 1978, ch. 2.)

In general terms, then, the aims of the 'education of the emotions' are to provide a suitable environment for the unfolding of the affective aspects of the person; it will involve the direction of impulse and feeling towards objects that will deeply satisfy, sometimes by way of eliciting new impulses and feelings, sometimes by channelling and redirecting them where they have fastened on less ultimately satisfying or inadequate objects; it will also involve taking steps to prevent occasions of emotional outburst; and over and above all this will be the endeavour to help children to take ultimate responsibility for themselves, not allowing themselves to become completely passive 'victims' of feeling or letting the life of feeling simply 'find its own level', but actively 'managing' their own inner lives as befits responsible persons.

How, then, are we to conceive of these tasks?

Teaching the Languages of Feeling: the Most General Task

Nearly all writers who have concerned themselves with the present topic have drawn attention to the importance of language. It might well be said that most of the aims of the education of the emotions could be summed up under the heading 'teaching the languages of feeling', provided we interpret the word 'languages' in a broad sense.

There are a great many ways in which we can look at language. But for our purposes the following are the most important.

(1) Language 'fixes' what was fleeting, dim and vague. As we have seen, experience at the 'endothymic' or 'pathic' level, at the level of pre-conceptual feeling-awareness, is hard to retain and hence identify unless it is 'captured' in concepts or some other 'fixed' medium. At this lower level we simply 'live through' our experiences. If we are to know what

our experience is like, *a fortiori* if we are to be able to 'manage' it by taking up some kind of position towards it, we must have some way of distinguishing aspects of it. Some kind of language is indispensable for this.

(2) Language helps us 'express ourselves'. Feeling itself 'presses on' towards some kind of termination in expression, in words, gestures, rituals, or other outwardly observable phenomena. If all life is a search for meaning – either for what means something to us or for what has meaning in itself – and we are soul-body unities, then this need of feeling for an objective termination is intelligible. It is a sign of our need to be whole, to act as wholes.

(3) Language enables us to communicate. We are essentially social beings, and cannot develop – at least in the early stages of our lives – without the society of other human beings. Hence our expressive media must be readily intelligible to others, so that we can come into psychic contact with them. There is a 'natural' language of gesture, and so on, but because of the 'open' nature of our 'instinctual' drives this has to be supplemented by 'cultural' languages, or languages that have to be taught and learnt.

(4) Language binds us together with some people and separates us from others. The effect of the first three aspects of language is to create language communities which experience themselves as separate from other language communities (see the myth of the Tower of Babel, Genesis XI: 1–9). But we speak many 'languages' and the important question then becomes: are there some languages that we all speak, and, if so, do they provide the same *depth* of shared experience that the more exclusive languages provide? If so, the sense of unity is capable of counterbalancing the sense of difference.

I do not want to imply that these four functions of language exclude each other. Where emotion and feeling are concerned they are closely bound up together. For example, a teenager may ask her friend why she is so silent and glum. The friend, who has perhaps not been consciously aware of this before, bursts out with: 'I'm fed up with school, that's why.' The use of 'the language of feeling' thus helps her realise something about her current state, provides a more adequate termination than mere silence, is a vehicle of communication and, because it elicits an answering feeling from the other girl, serves to bind the friends closer and sets them a little further apart from those who represent 'school'. We should note, too, that if the words 'I'm fed up with school' are spoken in a completely dead-pan voice, then either the girl is near despair or she is in some way *mis*using the language (Williams, 1965), and her friend will not know quite how to take them. Communication and expression are particularly closely bound up together (Benson, 1967, pp. 338f.).

89

Let us now survey the sorts of things that might be called the languages of feeling.

(1) The Specific Emotional Vocabulary

This comprises:
(a) words and standard phrases indicating or characterising feeling, mood, and so on;
(b) words characterising the world affectively.

The first sub-class of terms is extremely loosely used in ordinary life, and a great deal of disagreement and misunderstanding obtains with regard to the more recondite terms. An interesting classification of such terms can be found in Aschenbrenner (1971). He distinguishes the following classes of term: terms indicating 'satisfaction' and 'appetition'; 'direct responses' (to persons and things); 'situational affects' – comprising 'affects of causal involvement' (including confidence, hope, apprehension and fear) and 'cognitive affects'; 'responsional characterizations' – used to characterise others' responses and one's own past responses; 'moral affects' (several sub-classes); and 'diathetic characterizations' – used to characterise 'emotive tone and temperament'. But despite the great extent of this vocabulary it remains an exceedingly blunt instrument for those who wish to convey the precise quality of their feelings and leads people to talk of some emotions and feelings being unspecifiable (Warnock, 1957, p. 44).

One way of making up for this is to talk about the world in an 'affective' way. Swearing is a crude form of this, as is the comparatively mindless phrase 'it's great' for characterising things one is attracted to. But all value-terms, if used 'authentically' – that is, as a record of one's own experience rather than of a more general social accolade (or the reverse) – both characterise objects and convey something of how one is affected by them (examples are 'generous', 'shifty', 'graceful', 'vital', 'noble', 'stunted', 'self-indulgent', 'profound').

But again it is clear how very inadequate this vocabulary is in itself, even if supplemented by non-verbal expressive forms.

(2) Extensions of these Vocabularies through Metaphor, 'Poetic' Language, and so on

Even though it is a cliché, the phrase 'boiling with rage' may be a great deal more successful in conveying a person's state than 'very angry', since it emphasises the bodily involvement; 'very angry' has a 'bloodless' feel about, it, which, again, can only be compensated for by tone of voice and other non-verbal factors. But if it is part of the education of the emotions to encourage written accounts of emotion – as it surely is, since only then can a truly 'fixing' precision be attempted – the resources of language must be explored in their entirety. And, of course, one has to go to literature, especially great literature, to see how this is done.

(3) The Use of Quotations, Proverbs, Myths, and so on

If one's aim is to teach children to 'fix' their own feelings and express themselves one must teach them how to think, speak and write about emotion and feeling, or about the world-as-apprehended-through-feeling. But if one is concerned with the third and fourth functions of language listed above one can use literary works, together with proverbs, myths, legends and stories, as indicators of one's own feeling or as vehicles of shared feeling. The best-known quotations in common use express a cultural attitude to something, and the currency of quotations (stories, proverbs, myths, etc.) is a measure of the degree to which the feelings they express are shared in the language community.

(4) Language in General

Unless one's interests are purely technical and utilitarian the learning of a language inescapably involves initiation into a way of feeling. This is obvious in the case of a first language, less obvious in the case of a second, since most people never get much beyond the La plume de ma tante level. But the languages of the world split up the phenomenal field of emotion, feeling and mood in strikingly different ways, reflecting or creating (more likely both) the 'national character' of the language-speakers. The same is true, of course, within languages, of the various dialects, 'registers', slang-supplements, and so on, that serve partly to subdivide, partly to 'sub-unite', the members of linguistic communities from and to one another.

A note on reading aloud. Reading aloud to children is enormously important at all levels of their education. It should now readily be seen how reading aloud with plenty of expression is an essential part of teaching them how to feel. Through intonation, pauses, changes of pace and volume, indeed through changes of facial expression and even posture, the reader brings the words on the page to life and helps children to feel the significance and meaning of human situations hitherto foreign to their experience, learn how the human race in general, or the people of the Western world, perhaps, have learnt to respond to important events, and so on. They will not get a fraction of all this if they are always left to read silently to themselves. It is thus very important that teachers – especially first and middle school teachers and those of humanities subjects in secondary schools – are given a thorough training, where native ability is lacking. Children should also be taught to do it; if sympathetically done it can immensely increase their understanding of human situations. In being shown how to breathe life into the words on the page they come to understand them more deeply and inwardly.

(5)   Art and Music

It is almost impossible to deny that art and music are also in *some* sense 'languages of emotion' – however difficult it may be to account for this. All four of the functions of language picked out above can truly be ascribed to them. Indeed some writers, for example MacMurray, see the arts as the most important elements in the education of the emotions. What makes it difficult to account for their performing some of the functions of language is the paucity (perhaps total absence) of recognisable and repeatable *elements* that clearly denote some unit of meaning. Works of art are unique. But they seem to mean something in spite of their uniqueness, a uniqueness that cannot plausibly be interpreted merely as a unique combination of meaningful elements. Indeed, they mean something in themselves and thus cannot be translated into another medium. Clearly it is this that accounts for their deep significance. Mere *accounts* of emotion and feeling are always inadequate, because at the level of feeling-awareness, where the meanings of the world are directly borne in upon us, experience is 'qualitative' and unrepeatable. Yet ordinary language is a structure of general terms and general rules for their use. Attempts to describe experience thus always 'leave something out', and subtly distort what is conveyed. Only to the extent that 'mere description' becomes 'poetry' (in a broad sense) does language become adequate to convey the qualitative nature of experience. For poetry – and, we assume, because of their experienced kinship with poetry, art and music – does convey something of the felt quality of experience and, despite the uniqueness of individual works and the lack of repeatable elements, in so doing conveys something universally significant to us.

But though the artistic creations of others may convey universal meaning and significance to us they cannot always be completely adequate vehicles for our own subjectivity. R. W. Witkin ascribes great importance to creative activities in school because human beings sometimes need to express themselves in forms chosen to fit their *own* situations. He argues that we are obsessed with objective approaches to things, in which we let ourselves be determined over-much by the world outside us. To be whole, we need also to cultivate subjectivity. But it is not enough merely to accept our feelings and act appropriately, because the form of our action will be too much determined by the objective nature of things. In any case we only really know our feelings in finding an expressive medium for them. But art, which balances the choice of form (to suit our own situation) and the objective limitations of the medium (which provides us with our problem), provides the perfect answer, and thus enables us to express ourselves as whole persons with 'the intelligence of feeling' (the title of his book). Witkin's book (1974) is not easy, but is an important defence of the need for including creative subjects in the curriculum. It also abounds in practical discussions and suggestions.

(6) Gesture, Posture, Tone

I have already implied that the 'vocabulary' of emotion, and its extension in metaphor, story, and so on, is likely to be pretty ineffective – indeed, at performing any of the functions listed – unless it is spoken properly, with the appropriate tone and emphasis, gesture and bodily comportment. We 'fix', express and communicate our feelings most adequately and effectively as the body-soul unities we are, that is, without inhibition. Even works of art, through which the universal significance of our feelings is conveyed, normally require some kind of public or private 'performance' (real or imagined), involving the body. But there clearly are separate and distinguishable 'body-languages' also, and here the difficulty of demarcating what is natural from what is conventional is linked with the fact that our expression of emotion and feeling is not always deliberate. Some philosophers have wanted to talk about 'evincing' and 'betraying', as opposed to 'expressing', emotion in such cases (see Benson, 1967, pp. 339f.), but these distinctions are not easy to make, since the borderline between what is 'deliberate' and what is not is itself extremely shadowy.

(7) Customs, Manners, Rituals, 'the Done Thing'

Because of the importance of communication and community-feeling, human actions tend towards uniformity. The conventional 'form' that actions take invariably marks out something generally held to be important. Thus, whenever there is an issue of 'the done thing', one is being invited or expected to 'feel' in a certain way. Some customs, manners, and so on, are 'forms' taken by purely instrumental actions (writing letters, introducing people, signing contracts), others are mainly expressive, such as mourning rituals and ceremonies of initiation. The instrumental and expressive categories are, in fact, hard to separate except in a culture obsessed with means-ends thinking, as ours is.

(8) *Intellectual, Artistic and Practical Activities*

These are the activities that largely constitute the curricula of secondary and higher education. As Polanyi writes in his account of knowledge (1973, pp. 173f.):

> Scientific value must be justified as part of a common culture extending over the arts, laws and religions of man, all contrived likewise by the use of language. For this great articulate edifice of passionate thought has been reared by the force of the passions to which its erection offered creative scope, and its lasting fabric continues to foster and gratify the same passions. Young men and women brought up in this culture accept it by pouring their minds into its fabric, and so live the emotions which it teaches them to feel. They transmit these emotions in their turn to succeeding generations, on whose responding fervour the edifice relies for its continuing existence.

Science is thus a 'language' based on and prescribing feeling – not only feeling about what is worth studying, but also a feeling for 'intellectual beauty', which Polanyi argues is the main indication of scientific truth. The same sort of thing can be said of all intellectual disciplines, and all practical and artistic activities; of any activity, indeed, in which there is an issue of 'standards' and 'rules'. All of them not only prescribe feeling but 'offer creative scope' to existing feeling (provided, that is, that the 'rules' are ultimately treated as rough guides rather than masters).

It may now be clear how these various 'languages' or 'vocabularies' serve to fix, express, or communicate feeling and again to create community of feeling. But how do they *educate* it? If we closely tie the notion of education to that of 'rationality', interpreting the latter in terms of 'public forms of discourse', this question is virtually impossible to answer. But if we hold fast to the dynamic picture of the human being as a bodily-psychic unity striving from the first to develop itself, and see education largely in developmental terms, the answer becomes clearer. The various 'languages' of emotion are the 'forms' that enable the relatively 'open' and formless, if roughly 'directed', 'matter' of impulse and feeling to develop itself. There is no doubt that this is true of language in general.

A normal child will, as it were, 'expand into language' as he grows older even without his parents and siblings deliberately setting out to teach him. Language is *Lebensraum* for the developing person. And of course language in general brings with it ways of feeling, as we have seen. Again, if a bodily-psychic unity learns the 'bodily' *aspect* of 'expression' (though young children will be incapable of making this distinction of aspects), he will come to feel the feelings of which the expressive 'movements' or 'sounds' he has picked up (without, of course, seeing them as such) are the normal outward aspects. This, of course, continues to work with adults. If we act or read the part of a grief-stricken parent in a play, we shall feel grief for as long as we are 'in' the part (and its 'echo' may continue much longer). Indeed, if for some reason we are in fact feeling sad at a real event in our lives yet are unable for some reason to express our grief, we shall experience the play acting or reading as a relief.

The general principle is thus clear. The child strives (unconsciously, of course) to develop himself. The time comes when, say, cognitive strivings are stirring in him. But his home environment offers no 'creative scope' for their development. The teacher introduces him to and encourages him in cognitive activities appropriate for one at his stage of development. The child seizes on these activities as ways that 'answer' to his 'search' for something-to-take-a-cognitive-interest-in. Because the time is really ripe and there is no serious distraction to divert him he makes these activities 'his own'. The outward 'movements' (measuring things, perhaps, and writing the results in a book) become truly expressive of his own feeling-interest, and he gradually comes to 'feel' in the sort of way scientists feel.

The actual picture, of course, is vastly more complicated than this. His going through the outward 'movements' of cognitive interest, and so on, may in fact be his way of 'finding' the social recognition or the self-value he is also 'in search' of. Or his cognitive interests may have been seriously inhibited and repressed at an early age. Or the cognitive interests are too faint to outweigh his will to power over his fellow pupils. And so on. But the general point is clear. Introducing children to the 'languages of feeling' works because such languages are long-tested 'answers' to human strivings, 'forms' for the developing 'matter' of impulse and feeling, ways in which human beings can come to realise their own potential natures.

It must be stressed also that emotional development must work to some extent independently of being taught the languages of emotion. A good many impulses and feelings have 'natural' outlets in human behaviour, and these will be sought and found by the child without our needing to encourage him. It is in the area of transcending feelings that most of what we have said above is primarily relevant – though even here there must be many cases of creative individuals finding the 'objects' they are 'seeking' by themselves. All 'languages' of any complexity and sophistication must owe much to human creativeness.

A note on stages of emotional development. This should make us wary of any hasty talk about logical stages of emotional development. This normally turns out to be an argument to the effect that a child 'could not' experience a particular feeling, say 'pride', without possessing the concept of 'ownership', or something similar. But experience and experience-quality must be logically prior to concepts and conceptual relationships. This is not to deny that the *languages* of feeling may in many cases, as I have suggested, be themselves the catalysts for certain affective experiences. But this cannot be so in all cases, and hence it is unwise to assert too confidently that certain feelings are not possible before certain concepts have been learnt – assuming that the possession of concepts has something to do with the ability to use the words of a language. Nevertheless, there are examples of talk of stages that are not open to this objection. Martin L. Hoffman, for example, argues that altruistic motives and feelings could not develop until 'the other' is *experienced* as different from 'myself' (1976). This point is much the same as the one implicit in the progression between Lersch's three main themes of the endothymic ground. Clearly the developmental progression must be from impulses and feelings of pre-individual existence to those of individual existence to those of transcending existence; it could not intelligibly be in the reverse, or any other, order.

Bloom's 'taxonomy' of educational objectives in the affective domain (1956) has been much criticised by philosophers of education (e.g. Gribble, 1970), but largely for neglecting to set out the *criteria* for judging developmental progress. The complainants usually take for granted the truth of Peters's claim that the education of the emotions is 'inescapably a moral matter'. I have given my reasons for disagreeing with this. Where I find Bloom lacking is in his general conception of the affective domain. It is clearly regarded as on the same level as the cognitive domain, not as constituting a layer of experience foundational to thinking and willing, as I have argued. Then again there is little trace of the idea of development in its true sense of making actual what was before merely potential, or existing 'in germ'. Thus though there is a kind of 'logical' progress observable in the move from 'receiving' to 'responding' to 'valuing', and so on (those interested in these stages of affective development are advised to consult the 'Taxonomy', where the whole picture can be seen), the process of 'internalization', as the whole progression is characterised, does not in fact ring true to experience. What is lacking here, as so often elsewhere, is an adequate view of human being as a whole.

K. M. B. Bridges, in her often cited work on emotional development in pre-school children (1931), also devotes some attention to stages with regard to anger, 'distress and tears', 'fear and caution' and other fairly basic emotions. She found the stages (which not all children went through) characterised by a decreasing amount of brute physical manifestations and an increasing movement towards social acceptability and more instrumental behaviour. The main factor accounting for development, she found, was 'experience'. The account is, in general, of little philosophical interest.

Particular Educational Tasks

I return now to the question of education, and to the consideration of various particular tasks that have been or could be singled out for special attention by teachers.

(1) Changing Cognition

Bantock starts his discussion of educating emotion by suggesting that altering the cognition of objects may lead to a change of emotion where existing reponses are 'inappropriate' (1967, p. 76). John Wilson defines education of the emotions as 'helping [people] to become more reasonable in the sphere of the emotions' (1971, p. 1), and this includes helping them to a more correct understanding of their objects. He explicitly calls this 'knowing that' – that is, conceptual or propositional knowledge (ibid., p. 117).

How, then, would we proceed in the case of a girl who is afraid of mice? We perhaps assure her that mice are not dangerous, and produce a mass of evidence to back our claims. Perhaps the pupil assimilates all these facts, she now possesses the relevant 'knowledge-that', yet she still shrieks, climbs on a chair, and so on, when mice are released into the room.

We should recall first that 'knowledge-that' is a distanced, external kind of knowledge. I can pass any number of 'public tests', showing that my 'beliefs' are adequately backed, and so on, and yet still not *experience* things as really so and so. It might be, then, that the girl in our example cannot be brought to *experience* mice as harmless, despite our talk. If 'changing cognition' is to work, we might justifiably claim, the change must be such as to affect her at the level of feeling-awareness. In other words 'cognition' is not enough. It must be 'cognition-cum-evaluation', the two elements being in fact indistinguishable parts of one experience.

We should note, also, that our attempts to educate her out of her fear

97

may not work because it is not fear that she feels but, perhaps, disgust. It is in fact not uncommon for people to be brought to give up their *fears* of, say, cows or travelling by plane partly as a result of the presentation of relevant evidence. But disgust is far less amenable to a 'rational' approach, since it is not so much linked to some putative *property* of the object (that it may or may not possess) as to contact with the object itself. In fact it is generally characteristic of what Lersch calls feeling-movements of living existence that they are not subject to 'rational' control. This is much more a feature of feeling-movements of individual existence.

But let us return to the person who is afraid of mice. If it really *is* fear she feels then the mere factual assurance of their complete harmlessness, if imparted with genuine authority, may possibly work. Demonstrations of their harmlessness by trusted friends or 'significant others', or again by, say, white-coated experts, who pick them up, let them run over their bodies, and so on, is slightly more likely to be efficacious. But in general it is likely that only if they can be experienced in *positive* terms, as beautiful, interesting, or in need of protection, is one really likely to have a good chance of educating feeling by 'changing cognition'. But, as we have seen, this is really a case of feeling-awareness being driven out by feeling-awareness, of one *Gestalt* replacing another. One's hope in such cases is that, thanks to the dynamics of development in the person, the potential 'thrust out' towards a new experience of beauty, or cognitive satisfaction, or love, which are all deeply satisfying, strengthened by the expected bonus of feelings of self-respect, social approval, or whatever, may be sufficient to produce the requisite 'clicking into place' of a new 'picture' of mice.

(2) Refining Feelings

The main task indicated here is that of encouraging higher emotions and feelings. Bantock gives as an example the encouragement of pity rather than anger towards a cat that has damaged one's property. MacMurray talks about shifting the centre of feeling from self to world. Margaret Phillips says that the objects of educated emotions are 'progressively further removed from the self' (1937, p. 16). Peters also stresses the need to substitute self-transcending for self-referring feelings. Although Bantock is not wrong to call this the encouragement of 'ethically desirable' states of feeling, we can also see that the transition from concern for self to concern for the not-self is a developmental matter.

This strong repeated emphasis on 'refining' feelings, which suggests that, left to themselves, children will naturally gravitate to a largely self-centred life despite the existence within them (we presume) of transcending impulses and pressures recalls Lersch's claim that there is within all people a natural disharmony, to which there is no 'natural' resolution, between transcending and lower conations and feelings. It is as though there were a 'split' in the psyche, one half tending to sink downwards towards the easier and perhaps more 'natural' life of living existence and existence as an individual self, the other feeling a pull from a world beyond the self, which promises in the end a greater, if more costly and less 'earthy', satisfaction. These phenomena clearly illustrate the imperative necessity for man to 'take hold of himself' and intervene in the running of his own life if he is to achieve full development. It seems to me that Midgley, in her laudable effort to point up the similarities between men and animals, goes wrong at this point, trying to suggest that the 'conflicts' we sense in the life of animals are of the same order as the struggle between higher and lower selves in human beings (Midgley, 1978, ch. 11). But there is nothing comparable in the animal world to the serious *appeal* to a person to pull himself together and stop destroying himself; much more is at stake here than the mere future presence or absence of certain human satisfactions.

In many cases, therefore, the child needs help in embarking on the life of transcending experience, and above all in sticking to it during adolescence. For it is then, above all, with the development of the sexual drive and the growing importance of the question of self-identity, that the themes of living existence and of existence as an individual self threaten to drown the themes of transcending being. All these difficulties are greatly exaggerated by commercial pressures, and the allurements of teenage culture which, with few exceptions, tend unremittingly to divert the adolescent's attention from his transcending impulses (which become identified with adult 'squareness', 'stuffiness' and with repressive elements in life) and to encourage lower ones into prominence. A large number of personal and social factors, therefore, make it extremely difficult for the adolescent to subordinate his own immediate concerns to the world of 'value in itself' which lies around him. For there can be no true transcending satisfaction without a measure of respect and reverence, a degree of humility. All transcending themes require the individual to 'bow' or submit to the needs, requirements, evidence, beauty, demands, or value of something existing in its own right in a world of its own that, in a way, challenges his own self-importance.

Now in fact the 'human economy' is such that our motives for doing what we do are usually mixed. Nearly all our actions are answers to more than one impulse. And it may be that many of us could never overcome the gravitational pressure of the lower conations without exploiting this state of affairs. We know that many of our philanthropic acts, cognitive endeavours, possibly even religious practices, are heavily influenced by our desire for social recognition, power, or self-value. When this is blatant and obvious in the case of other people we feel repelled by the 'hypocrisy' of it, and it is clear that the sorts of activity devised by human beings to satisfy our transcendent strivings and to serve their objects would be completely corrupted if there were not *some* people who engaged in them for more or less 'pure' motives. But it is highly likely that some of the latter class of people *first* engaged in the activities for mixed motives, but then later came to 'purify' their motivation by approving in themselves the proper transcending desires and disavowing the desires for fame, or power, or wealth that accompanied them. Perhaps this process of self-scrutiny sometimes leads people to the reluctant conclusion that certain transcending motives are too weak to maintain their former involvement in knowledge, art, religion, social service, or whatever, and they abandon them. But in others the interests flourish, greatly to the health of the socially sanctioned activities or 'institutions' (universities, charities, churches, and so on) themselves.

Despite the dangers accompanying the policy, there can surely be no doubt that teachers should make use of the phenomenon of mixed motives in encouraging the development of children's transcending drives. A rigid Puritanism in this matter (there are signs of it in MacMurray), leading to the ousting of all competition, marks, stars and grades, all rewards in the form of special encouragement and approval on the part of teachers, and so on, might allow a few with especially strong transcending drives, and those who received the necessary encouragement at home, to flourish, but would seem likely to leave a large number of children without the special help, stimulus and encouragement they need to overcome the 'gravitational pull' of lower drives. The really important thing is to provide for ways in which the possibly resultant inauthenticity and even hypocrisy may *later* be overcome by creating an atmosphere in which individuals are eventually encouraged to take responsibility for their affective lives and, of course, by exploiting lower motives sensitively and wisely.

But it is clear that personal example and encouragement are crucial here. Margaret Phillips's investigations confirm this expectation of the enormous importance of personal influence (1937). As she says, 'a sentiment for a person is, potentially, a sentiment for his world', for what he experiences as significant, which presupposes some sort of feeling. Polanyi, in the passage quoted a few pages back, talks of 'young men and women brought up in this culture accept[ing] it by pouring their minds into its fabric', and throughout his work he stresses that all development depends on 'commitment' – a kind of unreasoning, because not clearly justifiable, trust. Now a child may be darkly aware of an impulse to 'reach out' for a transcendent 'object' that, he blindly feels, will afford him the satisfaction he seeks. But this involves risk, since the 'pay-off' will not come immediately, and there is a part of him, perhaps, that still craves for the security of the familiar. But the sense of security engendered by a significant adult, especially one he loves or admires, may help him 'commit' himself. Such commitment involves a reordering of his world. 'Other people' have long, perhaps, featured in his *Gestalten* as 'sources of useful service', 'objects to be bossed around', 'sources of recognition and praise', and so on. At some stage there has to be a revolutionary switch, so that new *Gestalten* form in which 'other people' figure as 'fellow citizens', 'people in need', or 'people who may make some unpredictable appeal to me'.

The leap of trust required for transcending existence may also be made possible by what Scheler calls *Vorbilder*, or 'personal models' (1973, pp. 572ff.), ideal person-types whose lives are centred on specific ranges of value, by whom the individual feels *drawn* in love to a willing discipleship. Such ideal person-types may be exemplified for a person by real or fictitious individuals, people of history or legend, alive or dead. Because they represent ideals they are 'larger than life', and have the requisite attractive power. Traditional 'scripture' lessons were often centred on them, and much history teaching of the recent past, featuring heroes such as Richard Cœur de Lion or Hereward the Wake, clearly served the same function of putting children in imaginative touch with personal models. These not infrequently caught the child's imagination, corresponding, perhaps, to the 'search-images' that function, according to Lersch, as scouts for the groping conations of the developing person, ready to latch on to what gives promise of answering them. Their significance here lies in their *personal* nature, which makes them fit objects for the child's love, having the power to draw out of him that shift of *Gestalten* that is necessary if there is to be any genuine advance from self to transcending being.

A brief word should be inserted here about 'authority'. We experience true authorities as people to be obeyed or followed. Of course we can 'justify' our choice of authority. At the level of thought we present cogent reasons for our preferences, and there is no reason to think that all such justifications are given in bad faith. Genuine reasons are conceptual crystallisations of inevitably partial aspects of our feeling-experience. But our experience of true authority (as opposed to 'the authorities' – persons generally recognised as sources of command or recommendation found to be 'legitimate') is 'pathic' or pre-logical. This is why de Jouvenel baldly characterised it as the *power* to sway another man's will (1957, ch. 2), since it is not in itself a matter of 'reasons'. Nevertheless, we do not experience authority as constraining us, but as rightly requiring our voluntary assent. But because it operates at the pre-conceptual level, where feeling, conation and cognition are indistinguishable, it is a resource of emotional education. Perhaps the properly correlative 'respect' is not as efficacious as love or reverence in inducing the leap of trust, but it must be reckoned as one 'psychic mechanism' through which transcending experience can be elicited and encouraged, and thus strengthened.

From the educator's point of view, then, 'authority' is a quality to cultivate and strengthen in himself, and its loss may signal the end of his real effectiveness. Its main emphasis is conative – de Jouvenel speaks of 'the ascendancy of a settled will which summons and orients uncertain wills' (ibid., p. 30). Thus nobody can be a true authority who does not know 'where he is going'. Hence the man of authority must be 'emotionally educated' himself, must have attained to a consistent and harmonious scale of value-preferences that enable him to attain a reasonable degree of satisfaction of all or most of his fundamental drives. Deep divisions in the personality, serious inconsistencies in behaviour, a number of basic impulses still experienced as clamouring in vain for satisfaction – all these things, which are signs of emotional immaturity, will also seriously undermine the natural expectation of authority that a child brings, social conditions allowing, to the 'grown-up' members of his environment.

(3) Channelling Affectivity into 'Socially Acceptable' Forms

This task is very prominent in the literature of our field. Bantock, for instance (1967, p. 81), gives an example of the teacher instructing children in good manners, so that instead of shouting 'shut up' in a crude and aggressive way at a disturber of their peace they come eventually to ask him politely to be quiet. This linguistic substitution may help people to contain their anger and thus modify it. This, of course, shows us why it is so important to discourage regular swearing, which is essentially an expression of, but may also be an inducement to, a gnawing hatred of the world.

K. M. B. Bridges (1931) puts a great deal of emphasis on the factor of 'social acceptability'. She is here a good representative of the line of thought that practically equates emotional with social development: 'Emotional development consists in the decreasing frequency of intense emotional responses, in the progressive transfer of responses to a series of stimuli determined by experience and social approval, and in the gradual change of the nature of the overt responses in accordance with social dictates' (p. 5), and then again, 'social desirability is the chief criterion of development', even though 'the criterion of social approval must necessarily be vague and arbitrary' (pp. 6 and 9).

Though Bridges vastly overemphasises the 'social' dimension, there is no doubt of the importance of channelling. Melville's story *Billy*

Budd contains an instructive episode. The hero, Billy, stammers badly. When he is falsely accused to his face of stirring up a mutiny on board ship the Captain, confident of his innocence, asks him what he has to say. Billy's stammer prevents him from uttering a word, and eventually his feelings, denied rational expression, become so strong that he 'says' what he had to say 'with a blow', which in fact causes his false accuser's death. Bantock is clearly right to draw attention to language as a resource of the first importance for channelling and containing feelings that might otherwise be socially disruptive or dangerous to individuals.

In school, as elsewhere, there is continual need to 'contain' the expression of self- and life-referring impulses to make possible the development of transcending ones. Competitive games, the prefectorial system of keeping order, a system of symbolic rewards for achievement, are examples of ways of containing and yet allowing the expression of the will to power, egoistic drives, and so on. Bullies can be given responsibility and strictly defined powers, privileges can be bestowed and forfeited for good and bad behaviour. Many of the traditional devices are despised today, and are perhaps impracticable in many schools. But they are cited here to illustrate the sort of thing that has proved effective. Strong drives and impulses cannot be completely repressed by some young people; it is therefore incumbent on the school, for the sake of the whole enterprise in which it is engaged, to find appropriate and harmless outlets for them.

But, as Peters points out, it is likely that many of these measures will not work unless at the same time the transcending life is encouraged. If, instead of lashing out with fists or feet, and then again with my tongue, I repeatedly 'count ten' as I have been taught, and politely ask the disturber of my peace to make less noise, there is likely to be trouble in the end unless I can also see 'the disturber' as a fellow human being who has his own difficulties and his own problems as I do. *Merely* 'channelling' or 'repressing' is, in many cases, unlikely to be effective. The emotional life must be developed as a whole. 'Increase in social acceptability' is *one* aspect of a well-organised affective education, but there are other considerations as well.

(4) 'Individualising' Feeling, Where It Is Inauthentic, Superficial and 'Cliché-Ridden'

R. W. Hepburn (1972, p. 485) puts much stress on

> ousting vague and imprecise or crude emotions by more specific, appropriate and discriminating ones; [on] preventing emotion-experience from stagnating – replacing jaded and repetitive habit-emotions with fresh and keen emotions, coupled logically to new individualized ways of seeing.

103

Hepburn is here talking about emotional or feeling-responses. The less these are genuinely responsive to what is really 'there' in experience, the more lifeless and 'dead' they become, eventually imparting this character to experienced life as a whole. Thus both Hepburn and MacMurray emphasise the importance of encouraging children to look and listen *for themselves*, to live more deliberately in and through the senses, taking reality in 'directly' as feeling-quality, not filtering it through the grid of second-hand concepts and ideas. They both point to the arts, to literature and painting, as spheres of activity and interest where 'first-hand experiencing' is a necessity for outstanding work.

Hepburn also talks about the poet's ability to present the emotional feel of complex situations not normally held at once in the mind in real life. In becoming aware of this, the implication is, the individual will be able to do the same in his own life, thus vastly increasing his sense of vitality, freedom and enjoyment, since he is no longer confined to conventional and moribund ways of experiencing. Thus, to take an example, one man at a concert may simply respond to the music. If he has heard it many times before his response may have become rather 'tired', or over-critical. Another person may combine his response to the music with a response to the, perhaps, comically ugly or amazingly juvenile players performing it; the beautiful music as performed by these players under these perhaps inauspicious circumstances may 'blend' in his experience to provide an incomparably richer and enlivening whole. This ability to get the most out of the varying situations of life is well worth encouraging and cultivating.

The same sort of thing is important in the moral sphere. Many people's moral judgements are conventional and 'dead' because the situations in which the act is performed are not grasped in their totality. Nearly all human situations are complex, exhibiting a variety of value aspects. Unless children are encouraged to take in and synthesise all that is really there under the aspects (moral, aesthetic, practical-prudential, and so on) that concern them, all value-responses, and value judgements based on them, will be crude and stereotyped, confined within the blinkers of prejudice or ideology. Vitality comes from the free response of the faculties to the world as it is. I do not mean to imply here that a conceptual grasp of a moral situation is to be avoided. It is essential at the level of judgement and argument. It is simply to insist on the dangers of premature conceptualisation and the often deadening effects of moral schemata.

But Hepburn also wonders whether the arts themselves do not sometimes 'function as high-class purveyors of stereotypes' (ibid., p. 494). There is no doubt that all attempts to refine or 'individualise' emotions incur the danger of encouraging superficiality and inauthenticity. This is an inevitable result of man's lack of wholeness and integration. It is always possible that 'going through the movements' of feeling-response will remain comparatively external. As we have seen, development of the higher life of feeling can be experienced as threatening. Not only may one be reluctant to 'bow' to something outside one, one may also wonder whether one has the capacity for a full response at this level, or fear the consequences for one's life as a whole if one gets 'drawn in'. Among the writers who mention inauthenticity and its dangers in education there is much difference of opinion as to whether it is right to risk the inculcation of merely 'surface' responses.

However, it is clear that one way to avoid it is by encouraging precision and accuracy of response, by gently discouraging cliché and getting children to respond as individuals. But, unless this is to provide another kind of threat, it must be done with great sensitivity and careful regard for the children's capacities. The dangers of inauthenticity are clearly balanced by the equally real dangers of drying up feeling completely, of inducing in the child the determination not to respond at all for fear of 'getting it wrong'.

(5) Encouraging the Emergence of a Community of Feeling

No society or nation-state can survive unless there is genuine community between its members. The idea that a modern state only needs to foster 'contractual' or legally defined relationships is a dangerous myth. But the sense of community is a product of a sense of shared *experience*. It is thus necessarily based on shared feeling-awareness.

Certainly community is automatically fostered by the existence of a common mother-tongue since, as we have seen, ordinary languages teach one how (roughly) to feel about things. But we live in a country where English is *not* the mother-tongue of a surprisingly large proportion of the inhabitants, and where 'cultural pluralism' is upheld as a social ideal.

Such pluralism will work if the various cultures of our society are in fact 'subcultures' subordinate to a 'superculture' that embraces them all. This was the state of medieval Christendom, which combined to fight the Crusades and repel the invading Turks. There must, in other words, be some aspect or level of life about which there is community of feeling, and this aspect or level must be existentially weighty enough to compensate for the fact that in other aspects or levels there is no community of feeling and hence a tendency for the subcultural groups to draw apart.

The same thing must be true of a school, or a 'house' or class within it. Community, the sense of shared life and shared fate, is impossible unless it is based on shared feeling-responses concerning certain things experienced as important. And education is impossible without community (see Dunlop, 1979, p. 52).

It will be clear that this requirement works against the 'individualising' requirement of education of the emotions, and the need to guard against the superficial, inauthentic response. But man is not just an individual; he is also a social being, and this means not that he merely lives harmoniously alongside other individuals but that he experiences the world to some extent as they do – especially with regard to certain aspects of the world. What is more, these 'aspects of the world' must not be remote from people's ordinary experience – otherwise not enough people can experience them as vitally important. They must be part of the very air they breathe. Once religion performed this function. Religious symbols were everywhere, the course of life was planned about the festivals of the church, the whole meaning and purpose of life was involved in them. The vitality and power of the religious idea to create community is shown by the fact that it still lingers on as a unifying factor today, despite almost centuries of widespread apostasy and indifference. The great problem with the many substitutes that have been proposed is their abstractness and lack of vitality, the difficulty of finding real material symbols of them, their inability to engage ordinary people's allegiance.

I raise this question without any intention of proposing a solution. The answer must lie somehow, I think, in religious education, as MacMurray thought, but it is exceedingly difficult to be sure what form it ought to take. A complete picture of man, however, and an understanding of the extent to which he depends on common traditions and shared experiences makes it overwhelmingly clear that a rough uniformity of feeling concerning the things that really matter is a necessity if he is to flourish. For how can I *trust* my neighbour, colleague, or partner if I cannot assume that he feels as I do about certain fundamentally important things? This requirement leaves much room for genuine individuality in many spheres, and allows for much differential emphasis even within the important areas. And any worthwhile society can afford to leave some space for the genuine eccentrics and non-conformists. But when all this has been said, we are left with the stark fact that societies and institutions dependent on community are not immortal, and that they do decay unless there is a considerable amount of shared feeling to uphold them and make them flourish. Individualism cannot be allowed to have the last word.

(6) 'Cooling' Responses and Encouraging the Formation of Sentiments

Margaret Phillips makes this the defining task of educating the emotions (1937, p. 16):

> Educated emotions are those which are integrated, or organized, in sentiments; which no longer function spasmodically, in isolation

106

or to conflicting ends, but rather work smoothly and consistently together, modifying and reinforcing each other in support of a common purpose. Such emotions are blended, as primary colours may be blended, to produce new and subtle harmonies, their individual strength and brilliance being subordinated to a dominant theme.

The 'raw material of sentiment formation', she goes on later, very much in harmony with the position defended in this book, 'is the "purposive striving" of the mind in contact with its world'. This striving involves awareness, activity and emotional colouring. Since the mind's purposes and the world are relatively constant, certain things become foci of effort and emotion, and thus sentiments develop. These are only theoretically distinct from one another. In practice they ramify, coalesce, interconnect, and so on. Much of ordinary life can be explained in terms of them (pp. 17f.).

Sentiments, then, give continuity and shape to life. As Findlay writes, wants having 'a development in coolness' lose their 'crude, immediate strength' and acquire 'the strength to persist . . . to channel thought and action in relatively sustained fashion' (1961, p. 179). Such 'long-term channelling orientations' become part of a person's *character*, and tend towards 'the wide generality of a fixed plan of preferences', which makes possible the sort of attention to detail and insertion of projects in the real order of things that spasmodic, warm wants often do not (ibid., pp. 183f.). The danger is, as Findlay goes on to point out, that 'the detachment of our cool practical life from the pulls and pressures of primary wanting . . . will also make possible the comprehensive, unreasoned *dis*regard for this all'. This can lead to 'caprice, recklessness and perversity' (p. 185) and, we may add, to wholesale inauthenticity.

Nevertheless, the need for the organising power of sentiments becomes obvious to us when we meet someone whose wanting is warm and enthusiastic, who feels deeply about things, yet never persists long in his enthusiasms or achieves any really lasting relationships with other people. It is clear that such a person's lack of 'character' results from a lack of wholeness and integration, from living too predominantly in feeling and impulse, without 'marrying' these to the 'higher' life of rational thought and will. The encouragement of sentiments can thus be the encouragement of wholeness.

Although Phillips is well aware of the dangers of inauthenticity – 'false' sentiments, she says, may result from attempts 'to force interest and attention prematurely afield' (1937, p. 310) – she argues strongly for the strategy of using the child's 'lower' and perhaps more 'natural' feelings as a ladder to 'higher'. In particular the teacher should try to encourage certain sorts of 'connection' in the child's mind, the most important of which link the approvable objects of sentiment with (*a*) persons for whom positive sentiments already exist, (*b*) the child's own self (so that he gets the idea of himself as a person with such and such interests, etc.) and (*c*) 'societies' for which sentiments already exist. Under 'general strategies' for encouraging sentiment-formation she includes especially:

(i)   provision of a rich and stimulating environment of potential objects of sentiments (these include personal models, ideals, and so on),
(ii) removal of all that may keep 'energy locked up in infantile purposes and interests', or give rise to too much interest in the self,
(iii) suggestion of links between the self and objects of interest that can be incorporated in the sentiment for the self.

(7) Encouraging Emotional Autonomy

This must be the culminating feature of any emotional education. The first thing to remember is that the 'self' who is to be encouraged to rule itself is not the will, or the 'reason', or the intellect or any other partial function or activity of the person, but the whole stratified person himself. Certainly there is in the human person a 'centre', an 'I' who initiates acts of willing and judging, and is aware of experiences 'arising' into consciousness. And it is to this 'I' that the commands 'know thyself' and 'take responsibility for your own personal development' are addressed. But this 'I' is not complete with its own 'rational criteria' for success in these enterprises; still less is it 'free' to *decide* what is to count as such success. Rather, it listens to the various 'voices' of itself, feeling its path towards the goal in ways that it cannot give a public account of.

Self-rule, or self-management, in other words, is a deeply mysterious thing of which no satisfactory account can be given, except in vague terms like 'maintaining a balance' between the strata, or 'integrating' the various 'parts of the soul', and so on. But it seems likely that if the *idea* of 'taking responsibility for one's own self-development' can be conveyed to people, and they authentically accept this responsibility, then they will succeed. The really difficult thing is to get over the idea that something like this is even possible – let alone incumbent on a person.

An obvious precondition of it is that the child should experience his own value or dignity – not as a person with such and such achievements to his credit, but simply as the person he is. It is vital, therefore, that teachers respect all the children entrusted to their care, and take them seriously as fellow, if junior, workers at a common task – that of working out one's own salvation, or fashioning one's own life.

The child must also be gradually taught that he *has a nature*, which it is his job to develop. He can only be enabled to accept this if, again, he feels valued and respected, if his dignity is not threatened. He must, again, be encouraged *to accept himself*. He might, perhaps, think it would be pleasanter if he were different, but since he is who he is, he can in fact only find true happiness and satisfaction within these limits.

Again, the child needs to feel strong in himself. He needs the confidence to live out of himself, without inducing inauthenticity in himself by aping his peers, or worrying too much what other people think of him. Children thus need to be quiet and silent at times; they need to be taught to meditate or pray or in some other way 'collect' themselves, and 'be with themselves'. In this way they can come eventually to feel the deep sources of strength within themselves, and resist the blandishments of a totally 'exteriorised' and 'outward-turned' life. Lersch argues that the encouragement of 'inwardness' is the only answer to the destructive and dehumanising tendencies of modern life.

But all this concerns autonomy in general. As regards affective autonomy, we must encourage the child neither to give way to every impulse or feeling that arises in him, nor to disregard his feelings and impulses. The key idea is expressed by Lersch: he must be taught that it is his task to 'take to himself' the *themes* of all his conations, and develop sentiments that order and harmonise them so far as he can. But he must above all take feeling *seriously*, having the confidence to 'live out of his feelings' where they can form a coherent basis for judgement and will. Above all, he must not let ideology, fashion, intellectualism, or a purely 'instrumental' life tempt him to *deny* his feelings, as is so common today, especially among the products of higher education.

G. D. Marshall talks about the power we have of opening and hardening our hearts (1968, pp. 250f.). This seems to me to involve approaching objects either with a willingness to be affected by them, to allow them to 'speak' to us, or alternatively with a refusal or a rebuff. The child needs to be taught to see the world as an inexhaustible treasure-house of beauty, interest and 'meaning', and again as a field for his action in an astonishing variety of hitherto undreamt of ways. He needs thus to be taught to see life as a field of genuine possibilities, and yet also, for he is a thinking being, as a real sphere for his own operation subject to laws that he cannot change. But, on the other side, he must also be gently shown the 'negative' side of the world, and the many 'blind alleys' it contains.

In all this he must be encouraged to find what he *really* wants, what gives him the *deepest* satisfaction, what most *thoroughly* satisfies him. It is not to be expected that all children will discover the answers to these questions while still at school. But it is the task of education to introduce these sorts of question into their minds, and to suggest ways in which they may later come to answer them. Above all, teachers can insist that they will in the end only find the answers by looking within themselves. In the whole question of emotional autonomy, as in the question of autonomy generally, it is far more a matter of *raising* the issues, and of teaching that they are not easy to answer, than of expecting school pupils to answer them. The point is that the questions are unlikely to be asked for the first time later. And if we force children to answer such questions too soon we encourage inauthenticity. It is *after* school, when they have entered the world of work and have married or are on the point of it, that the pressures of life itself make it more urgent that the questions should be answered. School is still, and should continue to be, a 'protected' environment.

It is important, too, that these attempts to prepare children for autonomy do not result in promoting self-*study* or introspection, which is largely an 'aesthetic' occupation. If people become too *interested* in themselves they become less capable of intervening in their own internal economy. The stress should be on responsible action; self-scrutiny, except in its purely moral or religious forms, should be more 'glancing' and incidental than direct.

These matters are not much written about today, certainly not in the literature of philosophy of education. There is no doubt much of importance I have omitted. The most important thing, it seems to me, is to give back to the idea of human being the dignity of 'royal rule', of getting children *used* to the notion that the 'monarch' (the 'I' who wills and judges) has to 'listen to' his subjects and promote their welfare, but is, in the end, the one who has responsibility for the whole, despite the fact that his own welfare depends on his subjects' efforts; that — and the idea of life as a *task*, most easily grasped in terms of self-development, of 'developing' and 'managing' the resources within one in response to the 'answering' goods of the world. If this picture of man could be once more taken for granted, the best ways of promoting it would, I am sure, soon come to light.

Factors Helping or Hindering the Education of the Emotions in School

(1) The Quality of the Teachers

In the long run teachers are far more likely to be effective through the example they set than through what they encourage their pupils to do, or what they indirectly promote in them. They *must* therefore be emotionally educated themselves, living fearlessly out of the heart of themselves, their feeling and striving fully integrated with their thinking

110

and willing. Above all, they must not be 'emotional misers', constantly inhibiting their *own* expressions of feeling (except on rare occasions), but emotionally generous (Tanner, 1976–7, has some interesting things to say on this 'most desirable of all human qualities'; see p. 139), imparting their own vitality to their pupils and taking away some of their fears of 'revealing themselves'. They must be serene, and have a ready sense of humour, to create or restore a relaxed atmosphere. They must let the love of their subject or subjects show in their outward demeanour. They must wish their pupils well, and have a steady affection for children and young people, because affective development (the foundation of intellectual and executive development) cannot take place properly in the face of hostility or indifference.

(2) The Atmosphere of the School

We saw above that feeling-states and moods have a foundational importance for feeling-movements and the rest of mental life. Thus the 'mood' or 'atmosphere' of the school, both as a physical environment and as an administrative and teaching community whose 'real' goals give it a particular kind of feeling-quality, are bound to affect emotional and other aspects of education. Some schools have a closed-in and depressing atmosphere, others an open and cheerful one; some seem dedicated to 'production' and have a dreary, 'mechanical' feel about them, others seem to promote growth and liveliness, and one catches in them a sense of the ultimate meaning of human life.

O. F. Bollnow stresses the need of the child to feel 'at home' in the world. School must offer him this sense of security, and the more it seems itself rooted – like the ideal home – in its physical and social environment, the more likely it will be to do this. Its atmosphere must be such as to awaken a cheerful mood in the child, to give him a 'morning' sense of future possibilities opening up, of life as full of promise. It must stimulate his sense of gratitude and obedience, his need to love and revere both his teachers and the 'personal models' his teacher holds out to him. It must enable the teacher to have confidence in the child, patience in relation to his task, hope for its favourable outcome. These things form the 'emotional *a priori*' of *any* genuine education (Bollnow, 1970, summarised in Vandenberg, 1975, pp. 35–7).

We have seen above that the great enemy of affective vitality is a predominantly technological attitude. This attitude has no use for 'love of the world', for reverence, wonder and awe, or indeed for any feeling whatsoever; it simply 'wants to get on with the job', bending its intelligence wholly in the service of its end. The sheer size of schools today, the growth of administration, the recruitment of men and women to organise rather than to teach, the adoption of 'management' techniques, and so on; all this leads almost inevitably to a depersonalising of school, to an overvaluation of efficiency and 'teamwork', to a reduction of educational goals to something clear-cut and obvious ('results').

By the same token it tends to make the traditional 'expressive' aspects of school seem meaningless, or feels compelled to give them a utilitarian emphasis. Assemblies cease to be conceived as occasions for expressing religious feelings, and are seen as devices for promoting social harmony and co-operation; speech days are no longer even ideally envisaged as times for showing forth love for the school, gratitude for its founders or providers, and respect for the learning and other achievements attained by its pupils, but as occasions for advertising the school, and 'justifying' it in the eyes of parents. This inability to understand the predominantly expressive point of rituals, ceremonies, festivities, and so on, is, of course, widespread in modern consciousness, but if we really wish to *foster* the affective life, and thus contribute to human wholeness, we must preserve or revive it. If we cannot ourselves see the point of it, it is because we are already too deeply dyed in the instrumental approach to things, or too alienated from the experience of community.

(3)   The Curriculum and Aims of the School

It has long been held important that children should receive a 'balanced' curriculum. But no amount of balance between mere subjects will be of much use if the teachers all teach their subjects in the same sort of way – that is, as purely 'objective', intellectual, or technical disciplines, in which the whole stress is put on conceptual understanding, forms of argument or justification, skills and techniques. There is no doubt that the examination system tends to encourage this sort of approach. But so does the 'social' interpretation of rationality I have repeatedly criticised, which underlies P. H. Hirst's 'forms of knowledge' thesis. Ultimately these phenomena are aspects of the technicising and instrumentalising of life that chiefly characterises our culture, and denotes man's flight from feeling and alienation from himself.

It is vital, then, that feeling is given its proper place in school subjects. As the quotation from Polanyi given on page 94 above indicates, there is much scope for feeling in the actual 'logic' of science, quite apart from the opportunities *teachers* of the subject have to express wonder at the natural world and love for and allegiance to their discipline and its demands. Technology, too, is full of scope for feeling. Solzhenitsyn, in *The Gulag Archipelago*, exclaims that Soviet-trained engineers 'could not hold a candle to the engineers of the older generation – either in the breadth of their technical education or in their artistic sensitivity and love for their work'. In all subjects the criteria of truth and rightness must ultimately be based on feeling-awareness, and in all subjects –

considered simply as guides to reality – a purely intellectual and impersonal, objective approach can lead to scepticism and nihilistic doubt. It is this sort of partial approach to things that has led to such widespread disbelief in God, though, in their hearts, all men continue to search for the Absolute. The courage to follow feeling, even though this always involves a leap of faith and a commitment, is essential in all life and is the first principle of rationality.

But subjects do also differ intrinsically in the scope they offer for the education of the emotions. The affective layer of experience itself is much more prominent in those subjects that require direct feeling-contact with reality, like the arts and crafts, or appreciative subjects such as literature. By contrast mathematics and science are essentially conceptual, and tend to replace the world we directly experience with an abstract world of ideas. Perhaps the most questionable subjects of all at school level are those that purport to deal with aspects of human being in an objective and impersonal way, like sociology and other social studies. Here the subject matter cries out for affective appreciation and feeling-intuition, yet far too often a deliberate attempt is made to repress this and man's life is filtered through a set of concepts that are only too often chosen not for their power to order and illuminate the human condition but because they serve some vague longing for social reform.

Let me finally make it absolutely clear that in my view the real dangers to affective education (and hence human wholeness) come not from the inclusion in the curriculum of practical themes as such, but from obsession (conscious or unconscious) with an instrumental approach to things. To tackle the planning of the curriculum with a realistic appreciation of the importance of work in human life and the consequent need to teach subjects that will be useful is not in itself to starve the affections and show an obsession with means-ends thinking; paradoxically, this is far more likely to come from a glorification of conceptual knowledge and forms of discourse as 'ends in themselves', because it is here that the feelings are suspect and the accent is on the employment of publicly acceptable arguments to establish one's title to 'knowledge'.

(4) The Attitude to Childhood

For good or ill, our age favours democracy and the attempt to treat everyone as an equal voice in communal decision-making. Our conception of society is increasingly 'associational'; relationships become more 'contractual' and less 'natural' and 'organic'; we are gradually becoming the rootless and soulless 'voting units' this way of looking at things suggests.

Naturally schools have not escaped these pressures. Many young and some older teachers enthusiastically promote the 'democratisation' of schools. But this, as I have shown more fully elsewhere (Dunlop, 1979), ultimately entails the equality of teachers and taught, and the destruction of the essentially hierarchical pedagogical relationship (see section 2 above). This is, perhaps, just compatible with certain sorts of training and the imparting of information and certain techniques, but it is quite incompatible – in its essence – with emotional education. The call to democratise schools is thus one form of the denial of the needs of childhood.

Related to 'democratisation' of the institution is the promotion of certain forms of political education, which require genuine participation in 'political' decision-making of one form or another. The effect of this is to make it much more difficult for children to enter into the themes of transcending existence, since political activity, despite its 'transcending' reference to ideals, thrives on the will to power and the drive for social recognition, which are essentially self-referring (see Dunlop, 1980, pp. 75f.). Politicians, or men and women who engage in political activity on our behalf, should only be trusted if they have had a genuine childhood, during which they have been thoroughly inducted into the civilising themes of transcending life. If politics is engaged in too early these conditions cannot be realised.

Another sign of our increasing inability to understand the needs of children is the tendency of teachers to expose them too early to horrors. Children must, it is thought, be made aware of the seamy side of life as early as possible; their literature must include 'realistic' and harrowing tales of bereavement and family break-up, they must be bombarded with pictures of children horribly mutilated by disease, malnutrition and war. But the effect of all this is either to blunt and cauterise feeling (the natural defence of the sensitive person to such 'overexposure'), or to engender a sentimental wallowing in feeling that has no appropriate practical outcome. Children must be taught to love the world, to open themselves to it and to hope for great things from it *before* they are deliberately introduced to its hateful aspects. Man cannot develop himself, cannot risk opening himself out to reality, unless it is clearly sensed that evil is merely the negation of good, the overturning of the normal order; to introduce children to good and evil at the same time and with the same intensity is to suggest that both are, metaphysically speaking, on the same level. This is not to say that children should be artificially shielded from *all* evil and suffering; many of them, perhaps most, can hardly avoid it. But I do suggest that our present practices are in some quarters in danger of amounting to an *assault* on children's feelings, which again takes little account of the real needs of childhood. Similar things must be said of some teaching methods – that they too quickly encourage the idea of children as simply small-scale 'rational' adults. Affective education is impossible unless the essentially hierarchical pedagogical relationship is encouraged, and children are regarded as in need of our help and protection.

(5) Popular Culture and the Quality of Modern Life

In writing this section I have been acutely aware of the fact that the school, whether it likes it or not, is to a great extent a reflection of the society or community it serves. Whether or not *we* try to produce a sense of hope in children, the world at large (with its television, unemployment, rampancy of the instrumental attitude and decline of community and family) will tend to cancel out our puny efforts. For what place is there in modern life any more for love, reverence, humility and quiet confidence in the forces of psychic renewal in the self? It is easy to get such a despairing impression from life if one leafs through a popular magazine, watches an evening's television, visits a hypermarket, or skims the newspaper headlines.

Real educators have probably always thought they were fighting a losing battle. There has always been a conflict between the ideals of good schools and many of the realities of the societies they served. This is merely a sign of human splitness and internal conflict, and of the need for constant renewal of the struggle to live rightly. But there are always good and hopeful signs too if one will take the trouble to look for them. For if man really *needs* to love, to look up to something or someone and to feel his own comparative smallness in the wonders of creation, he is bound to find a way of expressing this here and there.

The teacher, then, must see things in perspective. Knowing that all teachers have always felt their task to be virtually impossible, he must look for the good and hopeful signs in the world about him as well as the bad and apparently hopeless. Most teachers at first hope for too much. Later they tend to hope for too little. Both attitudes are unrealistic, and indeed are a sign of the teacher's own emotional miseducation. The teacher must learn to 'feel' for the good and the bad aspects of modern life, capitalising on the former and appropriately combating the latter. Above all he must have the serenity to carry on without being too much affected by what he hears on television and radio, reads in the papers, and so on, knowing that children are deep down much the same as ever, and that his task is to contribute in some perhaps quite small way to their development, and so help them to realise something of objective value and significance in the world.

6

A Final Note on Moral and Religious Considerations

At the beginning of the last chapter I argued that the education of the emotions was not 'primarily a moral matter', but a matter of helping children to develop themselves; that is, of helping them to make actual what was previously only potential and thus already in some way 'prescribed' by nature. Certainly the decision to do this involves valuational considerations, since it presupposes the idea that development is better than non-development. But this is not a *moral* preference in a thematic sense. A man who denies that development is better than non-development is not *morally* blind, like a man who denies that veracity is good or breach of trust bad, but 'ontologically' or 'metaphysically' blind, or just plain stupid.

However, a general consideration of the education of the emotions does reveal certain points of tension in the field, and the necessity for someone to choose between values that 'pull' in opposite directions, as follows:

(1) *'Natural development' versus the 'socially approvable' or, perhaps, the 'moral'.* For example, what *is* one's attitude to be about the drive for retribution of wrongs, or the feelings of disgust, envy, jealousy, or 'joy in another's loss of ease' (*Schadenfreude*)?

(2) *Authenticity versus inauthenticity.* Is it *never* a good thing to encourage inauthentic feelings in oneself, to please someone else, say, or so as not to 'cast a damper' on a social occasion?

(3) *Self-related versus other-related drives.* To what extent *is* it right to allow 'spiritual' achievements (writing a book, astronomical discovery, running the local branch of a charity) to be motivated largely by the will to power, or drive for social recognition?

(4) *Thought versus feeling as a general stance to life.* How far should one 'live in' one's impulses and feelings, and how far should one make the level of thought and will one's psychic 'centre of gravity'?

116

(5) *Receptivity versus instrumentality.* Is it really wrong to put a lot of stress on efficiency and means-ends thinking, planning, and so on, in one's life? Or is it really better to tolerate a lot of disorder in the material arrangements of life so as to make oneself more open to the unexpected, more 'available' to other people?

(6) *Autonomy versus 'passivity'.* Complete lack of autonomy seems to me an obvious case of someone failing to be a whole person. But how far should one be ready to 'surrender' to the mood of the occasion, say, or the spirit of the age? How far should one give in to stray impulses which, while not in any sense evil or likely to have obviously evil consequences, simply entail a readiness to be diverted from a previously chosen course?

These overlapping questions of emphasis clearly show that a merely species-developmental view of emotional education leaves a great deal of room for individual choice and social prescription. In actual fact there is a lot to be said for Pfänder's (1933) view that development also includes development as an *individual* person, as well as development as a person as such, and that the sort of position one should take on the various axes of tension I have pointed to are themselves obscurely indicated in the levels of satisfaction and frustration to be found from one's various attempts at forming one's own policy. Pfänder, indeed, claims that some people are expert at assessing the 'right' sort of positions for other people – that is, the positions that will enable them to develop their own individual natures most completely. Others might want to insist that such choices are moral choices, though Pfänder might have replied that they were so only in the sense that the question of whether or not to be 'true to oneself' was a moral question.

A much more fundamental challenging of the whole developmental approach might come from someone who took his stand on the basically religious idea that it was necessary to 'lose' one's life in order to 'save' it, and to 'deny oneself' and thus turn one's back on all developmental perspectives if one wanted to be morally perfect. Such a person might argue that the only morally justifiable course was to aim for the highest – for a life devoted entirely to self-transcending ends. Such a course would not necessarily entail ignorance of any of the valid points I have made in this book. It would rest on the acknowledged clash between the themes of existence as an individual self and those of transcending existence. It would accept that *some* level of self-preservation was necessary for complete devotion to other people, and so on, but it might argue that most of the self-referring conations should simply be denied.

The 'wordly' answer to this would be to insist that the 'higher' rests on the 'lower'; if there is disorder or undevelopment in the latter, the former cannot function fully or comprehensively. But this answer would ignore the interpenetration of the strata, and the principle of unity that binds them all together. A religious person might reply that alternative sources of strength and order are available to the 'ascetic', and that the normal laws of psychic life simply are not applicable once one admits the Divine into the picture.

Whatever we say about all this, we must surely accept that we are here within the realm of the supererogatory: nobody can be required by another person completely to deny his self-referring needs in this way. It must be a voluntary act of the individual. Indeed, I think we should be extremely wary even of 'recommending' various attitudes to the choices listed above except in purely developmental terms. We should, that is, regard them not as moral issues of the type where there is some 'educating' to be done, but at the most as issues where we can say words to this sort of effect: 'you, being the sort of person you appear to be, would be advised to do so and so' (e.g. follow your own inclinations more, think harder about your life, be less concerned with yourself, etc.). Thus, having at last raised the 'moral' question in this book, I am at once going to drop it. There is far too much moralising in contemporary philosophical writing on education. It is more important to get people to confront their *own* responsibility for making these broad choices.

Since, however, I have given a few hints about religious impulses and their proper object in the course of this book, I had better end by making my own position more clear. I entirely accept the general idea that our feelings are our guide to reality. This means that we must take religion seriously. For not only do we find within ourselves religious *conations*; some of us also find that a commitment to religious *practices* (worship and prayer) is not only satisfying in the long run – signalling that our conations have found the goal they were blindly seeking – but satisfying in a culminating or crowning fashion, as testifying to the presence or nearness of some Absolute object that brings *ultimate* satisfaction.

It seems to me that some kind of theism is also implicit in other aspects of the general position advocated here. For the whole idea of putting one's trust in feeling, in something whose operations are obscure, fleeting and occasionally quite misleading, seems preposterous unless one has reason to think that one's feelings or one's nature are themselves the creation of, and directly dependent on, something more obviously worth trusting. There seem, then, to be two alternatives (since feeling itself *has* to be relied on). Either one trusts in life, or in God. The problem about 'life' is that it seems to give rise – in the higher reaches of the human psyche – to something that gives itself to us as outside life, as belonging to some 'ideal' realm. I am referring, of course, to 'ideas' and 'values', to 'meaning' and 'significance' in general. And again, some of our conations are themselves directed to what is outside or beyond life, or has eternal significance. 'Love', for instance, gives itself to us as 'for ever'. How could this be if it were merely the product of perpetual change and decay (for let no one deceive himself into thinking that development is eternal)?

Trust in one's own feelings, then, seems itself to point to trust in a being who created our feelings and is the source of the life that wells up from our depths. That was also the conclusion of our, or Strasser's, discussion of passion (see above, pp. 84–6). I am not putting this forward as a 'proof' for the existence of God; indeed, I do not think there are any. But it does seem to me that reflection on human experience, especially our affective experience, and our need to trust it can lead one to realise that one has 'known' God's presence and existence all one's life, and has been trusting Him without perhaps recognising Him.

I want to end by recording my conviction that trust in reason as a social possession (which is a different position from the one that says we cannot do without the *guidance* and *help* of others if we would be rational) results from a *denial* of God. For if we no longer believe in Him we can no longer believe in ourselves, and have to invent some independent object called Reason (deified in France in 1793) as a substitute. But there is no *life* in an abstraction. Sooner or later we have to come back to a trust in our own feelings (drawing the proper conclusion from this) or perish.

Bibliographical Survey

The following list of books and articles includes all the works mentioned in the text, together with others that were consulted and found useful. I have not included a number of the more technical philosophical publications and some psychological works. In order to make it more useful as a guide to further reading I have added two sets of symbols. Asterisks indicate what I consider to be the more useful works I have seen, the most useful of which are indicated by two. The capital As, Bs and Cs indicate the general area(s) of interest touched on in the work, A standing for the general question of human nature, B for the nature of the affective sphere and its subdivisions, and C for educational questions. The allocation of these symbols could not be carried out without a slight amount of arbitrariness creeping in, as is virtually inevitable in such classifications.

B	Aristotle, *Rhetoric*.
**AB	Arnold, M. (ed.) (1968), *The Nature of Emotion* (Harmondsworth: Penguin).
**ABC	Arnold, M. (ed.) (1970), *Feelings and Emotions: The Loyola Symposium* (New York: Academic Press).
*B	Arnold, M. B., and Gasson, J. A. (1954), 'Feelings and emotions as dynamic factors in personal integration', in Arnold (ed.), 1968.
*B	Aschenbrenner, K. (1971), *The Concepts of Value* (Dordrecht: Reidel).
B	Baensch, O. (1923–4), 'Art and feeling', in S. K. Langer (ed.), *Reflections on Art* (Baltimore, Md: Johns Hopkins University Press, 1958), pp. 10–36.
*C	Bantock, G. H. (1967), 'The education of the emotions', in *Education, Culture and the Emotions* (London: Faber), pp. 65–86.
B	Bedford, E. (1956–7), 'Emotions', in D. Gustafson (ed.), *Essays in Philosophical Psychology* (London: Macmillan, 1967), pp. 77–98.
B	Benson, J. (1967), 'Emotion and expression', *Philosophical Review*, vol. 76, pp. 335–57.
AB	Bergson, H. (1935), *The Two Sources of Morality and Religion*, trans. R. A. Audra and C. Brereton (London: Macmillan).
C	Bloom, B. S. (1964), *Taxonomy of Educational Objectives, Handbook II: Affective Domain* (London: Longman).
**AB	Bollnów, O. F. (1941), *Das Wesen der Stimmungen* (Frankfurt: Klostermann).
**C	Bollnow, O. F. (1970), *Die pädagogische Atmosphäre*, 4th edn (Heidelberg: Quelle & Mayer).
*C	Bonnett, M. (1978), 'Authenticity and education', *Journal of Philosophy of Education*, vol. 12, pp. 51–62.
C	Bridges, K. M. B. (1931), *The Social and Emotional Development of the Pre-School Child* (London: Kegan Paul, Trench & Trübner).
B	Cannon, W. B. (1927), 'The James–Lange theory of emotion', in Arnold (ed.), 1968.
*B	Claparède, E. (1928), 'Feelings and emotions', in Arnold (ed.), 1968.

A   Comfort, A. (1966), *Nature and Human Nature* (Harmondsworth: Penguin).

A   Dent, N. (1974), 'Duty and inclination', *Mind*, vol. 83, pp. 552–70.

B   Descartes, R. (1649), *The Passions of the Soul*.

B   Duffy, E. (1941), 'An explanation of "emotional" phenomena without the use of the concept "emotion" ', in Arnold (ed.), 1968.

B   Dumas, G. (1948), 'Emotional shocks and emotions', in Arnold (ed.), 1968.

AC   Dunlop, F. N. (1977), 'Human nature, learning and ideology', *British Journal of Educational Studies*, vol. 25, no. 3, pp. 239–57.

AC   Dunlop, F. N. (1979), 'On the democratic organization of schools', *Cambridge Journal of Education*, vol. 9, no. 1, pp. 43–54.

C   Dunlop, F. N. (1980), 'On separating moral from political education', *Journal of Further and Higher Education*, vol. 4, no. 2, pp. 73–81.

A   Dunlop, F. N. (1982), 'Male and female: a prolegomenon to the question of educational sex-bias', *Journal of Philosophy of Education*, vol. 16, no. 2, pp. 209–22.

C   Ewing, A. C. (1957), 'The justification of emotions', *Proceedings of the Aristotelian Society*, supp. vol. 31, pp. 59–74.

*AB   Fell, J. P. (1965), *Emotion in the Thought of Sartre* (New York: Columbia University Press).

C   Findlay, J. N. (1954), 'The justification of attitudes', *Mind*, vol. 63, pp. 145–61.

**AB   Findlay, J. N. (1961), *Values and Intentions* (London: Allen & Unwin).

B   Findlay, J. N. (1963), *Meinong's Theory of Objects and Values* (London: OUP).

A   Forster, E. M. (1954), 'The Machine Stops', in *Collected Short Stories* (Harmondsworth: Penguin).

B   Green, O. H. (1972), 'Emotions and belief', in N. Rescher (ed.), *Studies in the Philosophy of Mind* (Oxford: Blackwell).

C   Gribble, J. H. (1970), 'Pandora's box: the affective domain of educational objectives', *Journal of Curriculum Studies*, vol. 2, no. 1, pp. 11–24.

B   Hamlyn, D. W. (1978), 'The phenomena of love and hate', *Philosophy*, vol. 53, pp. 5–20.

AB   Hampshire, S. (1951), *Spinoza* (Harmondsworth: Penguin).

*B   Hepburn, R. W. (1965), 'Emotions and emotional qualities', in C. Barrett (ed.), *Collected Papers on Aesthetics* (Oxford: Blackwell), pp. 185–98.

**C   Hepburn, R. W. (1972), 'The arts and the education of feeling and emotions', in R. F. Dearden, P. H. Hirst and R. S. Peters (eds), *Education and the Development of Reason* (London: Routledge & Kegan Paul), pp. 484–99.

**AB   Hillman, J. (1960), *Emotion: A Comprehensive Phenomenology of Theories and their Meanings for Therapy* (London: Routledge & Kegan Paul).

C   Hirst, P. H., and Peters, R. S. (1970), *The Logic of Education* (London: Routledge & Kegan Paul).

C   Hoffman, M. L. (1976), 'Empathy, role taking, guilt and development of altruistic motives', in T. Lickona (ed.), *Moral Development and Behaviour* (New York: Holt, Rinehart & Winston), pp. 124–43.

B   Hume, David (1738), *A Treatise of Human Nature*, bk II, 'Of the passions'.

B   James, W. (1884), 'What is an emotion?', in Arnold (ed.), 1968.

AB   James, W. (1950), *The Principles of Psychology*, Vols I and II (New York: Dover).

A   Jouvenel, B. de (1957), *Sovereignty*, trans. J. F. Huntington (Cambridge: CUP).

*B   Kenny, A. (1963), *Action, Emotion and Will* (London: Routledge & Kegan Paul).

*B   Klages, L. (1950), 'The life of feeling', in Arnold (ed.), 1968.

AB   Kolnai, A. (1974), *Der Ekel*, reprint (Tübingen: Max Niemeyer).

*AB   Krueger, F. (1928), 'The essence of feeling', in Arnold (ed.), 1968.

B   Langer, S. K. (1953), *Feeling and Form* (London: Routledge & Kegan Paul).

**AB   Langer, S. K. (1967), *Mind: An Essay in Human Feeling* (Baltimore, Md: Johns Hopkins University Press).

B   Leeper, R. W. (1948), 'A motivational theory of emotion to replace "Emotion as disorganized response" ', in Arnold (ed.), 1968.

B   Leeper, R. W. (1963), 'The motivational theory of emotion', in Arnold (ed.), 1968.

B   Lehmann, A. (1914), 'Theory of affectivity', in Arnold (ed.), 1968.

**AB   Lersch, P. (1954), *Aufbau der Person*, 6th edn (Munich: Johann Ambrosius Barth).

*AC   Lewis, C. S. (1978), *The Abolition of Man* (Glasgow: Collins).

*B   Lyons, W. (1980), *Emotion* (Cambridge: CUP).

B   McDougall, W. (1928), 'Emotion and feeling distinguished', in Arnold (ed.), 1968.

**ABC   MacMurray, J. (1935a), *Reason and Emotion* (London: Faber).

**ABC   MacMurray, J. (1935b), *Freedom in the Modern World*, 2nd edn (London: Faber).

*B   Marshall, G. D. (1968), 'On being affected', *Mind*, vol. 77, pp. 243–59.

A   Maslow, A. H. (1968), *Toward a Psychology of Being* (New York: Van Nostrand Reinhold).

B   Melden, A. I. (1969), 'The conceptual dimensions of emotions', in T. Mischel (ed.), *Human Action* (New York: Academic Press), pp. 199–220.

**A   Midgley, M. (1978), *Beast and Man: The Roots of Human Nature* (Hassocks: Harvester).

C   Mounier, E. (1956), *The Character of Man*, trans. and abridged C. Rowland (London: Rockliff).

B   Osborne, H. (1963), 'The quality of feeling in art', *British Journal of Aesthetics*, vol. 3, no. 1, pp. 38–53.

**AB   Peters, R. S. (1961–2), 'Emotions and the category of passivity', *Proceedings of the Aristotelian Society*, vol. 62, pp. 117–34.

C   Peters, R. S. (1966), *Ethics and Education* (London: Allen & Unwin).

**ABC   Peters, R. S. (1970), 'The education of the emotions', in R. S. Peters, *Psychology and Ethical Development* (London: Allen & Unwin, 1974), pp. 174–92.

**ABC   Peters, R. S. (1971), 'Reason and passion', in R. S. Peters, *Psychology and Ethical Development* (London: Allen & Unwin, 1974), pp. 151–73.

*ABC   Pfänder, A. (1922, 1930), *Zur Psychologie der Gesinnungen*, reprints (Halle: Max Niemeyer).

**A   Pfänder, A. (1933), *Die Seele des Menschen* (Halle: Max Niemeyer).

**C   Phillips, M. (1937), *The Education of the Emotions through Sentiment Development* (London: Allen & Unwin).

B   Pitcher, G. (1965), 'Emotion', *Mind*, vol. 74, pp. 326–46.

A   Plato, *Phaedrus*.

B   Plutchik, R. (1962), 'The evolutionary basis of emotional behaviour', in Arnold (ed.), 1968.

B   Plutchik, R. (1980), *Emotion: A Psychoevolutionary Synthesis* (New York: Harper & Row).

**AC   Polanyi, M. (1973), *Personal Knowledge* (London; Routledge & Kegan Paul).

*B   Pradines, M. (1958), 'Feelings as regulators', in Arnold (ed.), 1968.

C   Prescott, D. A. (1938), *Emotion and the Educative Process* (Washington, DC: American Council for Education).

C   Rawls, J. (1972), *A Theory of Justice* (London: OUP).

*AB   Reid, L. A. (1976), 'Feeling and aesthetic knowing', *The Journal of Aesthetic Education*, vol. 10, nos 3 and 4, pp. 11–17.

**AB   Reid, L. A. (1976–7), 'Feeling, thinking, knowing', *Proceedings of the Aristotelian Society*, vol. 77, pp. 165–82.

A   Reid, Thomas (1788), *Essays on the Active Powers of the Human Mind*.

A   Reiner, H. (1974), *Die Grundlagen der Sittlichkeit* (Meisenheim am Glan: Anton Hain).

B   Ryle, G. (1963), *The Concept of Mind* (Harmondsworth: Penguin).

**AB   Sartre, J.-P. (1948), *The Emotions: Outline of a Theory*, trans. B. Frechtman (New York: Philosophical Library).

*B   Scheffler, I. (1977), 'In Praise of the Cognitive Emotions', *Teachers College Record*, vol. 79, no. 2, pp. 171–86.

**A   Scheler, M. (1954), *The Nature of Sympathy*, trans. P. Heath (London: Routledge & Kegan Paul).

*A   Scheler, M. (1961), *Man's Place in Nature*, trans. H. Meyerhoff (New York: Noonday).

**AB   Scheler, M. (1973), *Formalism in Ethics and Non-Formal Ethics of Values*, trans. M. S. Frings and R. L. Funk (Evanston, Ill.: Northwestern University Press).

*C   Schrag, F. (1972), 'Learning what one feels and enlarging the range of one's feelings', *Educational Theory*, vol. 22, pp. 382–94.

*C   Schrag, F. (1973), 'Learning and the expression of emotion', *Studies in Philosophy and Education*, vol. 8, no. 1, pp. 30–51.

B   Shand, A. F. (1914), 'The nature of emotional systems', in Arnold (ed.), 1968.

B   Shibles, W. (1974), *Emotion: The Method of Philosophical Therapy* (Whitewater, Wis.: Language Press).

*AB   Smith, Q. (1977), 'Scheler's stratification of emotional life and Strawson's person', *Philosophical Studies*, vol. 25, pp. 103–27.

*ABC   Solomon, R. C. (1976), *The Passions* (Garden City, NY: Doubleday Anchor).

AB   Spinoza, B. de (1677), *Ethics*.

**A   Stein, E. (1970), *On the Problem of Empathy*, trans. W. Stein (The Hague: Nijhoff).

*A   Strasser, S. (1969), *The Idea of Dialogal Phenomenology* (Pittsburgh, Pa: Duquesne University Press).

**AB   Strasser, S. (1970), 'Feeling as basis of knowing and recognizing the other as an ego', in Arnold (ed.), 1970.

**AB   Strasser, S. (1977), *Phenomenology of Feeling*, trans. R. E. Wood (Pittsburgh, Pa: Duquesne University Press).

B   Strongman, K. T. (1973), *The Psychology of Emotion* (London: Wiley).

**B   Tanner, M. (1976–7), 'Sentimentality', *Proceedings of the Aristotelian Society*, vol. 77, pp. 127–47.

B   Trigg, R. (1970), *Pain and Emotion* (London: OUP).

*C   Vandenberg, D. (1975), 'Openness: the pedagogic atmosphere', in D. Nyberg (ed.), *The Philosophy of Open Education* (London: Routledge & Kegan Paul), pp. 35–57.

C   Warnock, M. (1957), 'The justification of emotions', *Proceedings of the Aristotelian Society*, supp. vol. 31, pp. 43–58.

B   White, A. R. (1967), *The Philosophy of Mind* (New York: Random House).

B   Williams, B. A. O. (1965), *Morality and the Emotions* (London: Bedford College).

*C   Wilson, J. (1971), *Education in Religion and the Emotions* (London: Heinemann).

**C   Witkin, R. W. (1974), *The Intelligence of Feeling* (London: Heinemann).

Notes to Supplement the Classified List and Indications in the Text

The affective sphere is one where the great 'classic' philosophers of the past have relatively little to contribute, partly because the systematic philosophical study of man is of comparatively recent growth and partly because of the difficulty of discovering what phenomena they were actually writing about.

Strasser (1977), Lyons (1980), Kenny (1963) and Hillman (1960) refer to and discuss them here and there in their books, and there are books such as Hampshire (1951, ch. 4) which may also be found useful. But in general references are few, and I shall not mention any classic philosopher in the following brief notes.

(1) Human Nature in General

Emotion, feeling, and so on, can only be made intelligible within a general survey of 'the human economy'. Much of the best work is foreign and still untranslated. But Strasser's work (see especially 1977) is increasingly available, as is Scheler's. The latter's *Nature of Sympathy* (1954) and *Formalism in Ethics* (1973) are extremely important. So is Stein's *On the Problem of Empathy* (1970). But continental thinking is difficult for those trained in an English academic environment. This is possibly why Polanyi (1973 and other works) is still grossly neglected, despite his outstanding importance. All this means that the English student would be recommended to start with Midgley, whose *Beast and Man* (1978) starts to fill an enormous gap in the English coverage of this major philosophical theme. Langer (1967), whose coverage of the human sciences is even wider than Midgley's and who is in essential harmony with her, is more difficult, as is Findlay (1961). But Fell's book *Emotion in the Thought of Sartre* (1965) is clearly and simply written, as is that of Solomon (1976), and both these writers put the Affective in a wide human context. MacMurray (1935a) writes simply and clearly, and his work should also prove very useful to students. Lewis's little book (1978) is also highly to be recommended, and Comfort (1966) may also be found useful. I cannot resist ending this section with a mention of E. M. Forster's short story 'The Machine Stops', which is a prophetic statement of what happens when the layer of feeling is sacrificed on the altar of technical intelligence.

(2) The Nature of the Affective Sphere

One of the best representatives of the English analytic tradition is R. S. Peters (1961–2, 1970, 1971, etc.). Kenny (1963), Bedford (1956–7) and Ryle (1963) are also to be recommended under this heading. An excellent and clearly written survey of theories of emotion by a recent English philosopher is Lyons (1980). The best phenomenological analysis of the sphere is Strasser (1977), supplemented by his 1970 paper. Hillman's exhaustive survey of theories of emotion (1960) is also written from this point of view. These two books are perhaps the most important full-length works available in English on the nature of emotion, feeling, and so on. But Strasser has the edge on Hillman because of his attempts to distinguish between different affective phenomena and his wider outlook. Sartre's book on emotion (1948) is also very important, though of limited scope. Other more or less phenomenological works specially to be recommended are Marshall (1968), Reid (1976–7) and Scheffler (1977). But of all these Strasser is the author one can least afford to dispense with, despite his relative difficulty (not helped by the translation, one suspects, though the introductory essay by the translator is very useful).

Mention must also be made here of Magda Arnold's excellent collections (1968 and 1970), and of Plutchik's survey of psychological theories (1980). Tanner's article on sentimentality (1976–7) is also important, as are the works of Findlay, which stress the vital connection of values with affectivity (1961, 1963).

(3) The Education of the Emotions

Recent philosophy of education in English-speaking countries has been strongly influenced by R. S. Peters, and the effect of his important 1970 paper has been great. But it should not be allowed to overshadow the contributions of MacMurray (1935a) and Phillips (1937); these are clearly and simply written, and to be highly recommended. By contrast the well-known work of Bridges (1931) is disappointing. So are Bloom (1964) and Prescott (1938), though both contain useful practical discussions here and there.

Among recent papers Hepburn (1972) seems to me to be outstanding; Schrag (1972 and 1973) is useful and clear, as is Bantock (1967). Wilson's book (1971) is much better in its practical suggestions than its theoretical underpinning, but is often very helpful. Witkin's contribution (1974) is impressive. If one can patiently master his semi-technical terminology one discovers something of great value. Also important are Bollnow's work on the affective climate or atmosphere requisite for education (1970), usefully summarised by Vandenberg (1975), and Bonnett's paper on authenticity in education (1978), especially the opening and closing sections. By contrast, much of the work on the justification of emotions, attitudes, and so on, seems to miss what is of real importance, besides being beyond the main scope of this book. But, in conclusion, the reader may once again be directed towards the work of Polanyi. Although he does not write primarily about education, let alone affective education, almost all his work has a direct bearing on the subject.

Index

(Excluding proper names that only occur in the bibliographical list, and general terms such as 'feeling', 'emotion', 'the Affective', etc.)